Contemporary Dance in the Low Countries

Published by the Flemish – Netherlands Foundation
Stichting Ons Erfdeel

Contemporary Dance in the Low Countries

Isabella Lanz and Katie Verstockt

This book is published by the Flemish-Netherlands Foundation 'Stichting Ons Erfdeel', which also publishes the following:
- *Ons Erfdeel, Vlaams-Nederlands cultureel tijdschrift*
- *Septentrion. Arts, lettres et culture de Flandre et des Pays-Bas*
- *the yearbook The Low Countries. Arts and Society in Flanders and the Netherlands*
- *the bilingual yearbook De Franse Nederlanden - Les Pays-Bas Français*,
and a series of books in different languages covering various aspects of the culture of the Low Countries.

Address of the Editorial Board and the Administration:

'Stichting Ons Erfdeel vzw', Murissonstraat 260, B-8930 Rekkem,
tel.: +32 (0)56 41 12 01, fax +32 (0)56 41 47 07
e-mail: red@onserfdeel.be   adm@onserfdeel.be
http://www.onserfdeel.be
VAT: BE 410.723.635

Head of Administration: Bernard Viaene
Administrative Secretaries: Adinda Houttekier and Hans Verhaeghe

Copyright © 2003 by 'Stichting Ons Erfdeel vzw'
Statutory deposit no.: D / 2003 / 3006 / 4
ISBN 90 - 75862 - 63 - 6
NUR 675
C.I.P. Koninklijke Bibliotheek Albert I

Cover: Geert Setola
Lay-out: Kees Nieuwenhuijzen - Geert Setola
Printed by: Die Keure, Bruges

This publication was produced in conjunction with the **National Lottery** (Brussels), the **Ministerie van Onderwijs, Cultuur en Wetenschappen** (Zoetermeer, the Netherlands) and the **Stichting Fonds voor de Podiumkunsten** (The Hague).

This book presents a picture of the dance scene as it currently stands in the Netherlands and Flanders. It takes the form of two general introductions and twenty portraits: twelve of Dutch choreographers and eight of Flemish. A separate chapter provides a brief look at companies, festivals, dance courses and dance workshops.

Dance has its own dynamic. Dancers, choreographers and companies are rarely tied to particular places or origins. Language makes little difference. *Contemporary Dance in the Low Countries* means dance that takes place in the Netherlands, Flanders *and* Brussels.

Although this publication cannot and is not intended to provide complete coverage, the aim has certainly been to give a representative outline of dance as it is in the Netherlands and Flanders today. The choice of choreographers and dance organisations covered is a matter of the individual preferences of the two compilers.

Isabella Lanz wrote the Dutch section, and Katie Verstockt the Flemish. The book is being published simultaneously in six languages: Dutch, French, German, English, Spanish and Italian.

The Editors

Contents

A VARIED LANDSCAPE:

DANCING FROM ABSTRACTION TO EXPRESSION AND BACK AGAIN

There is a fine photo of the moment itself. The audience is peering eagerly at itself in a large mirror. Nothing is actually happening on stage, there's no sign of any dancing. The setting for this performance (or lack of it) is the *Amsterdamse schouwburg* in June 1967. If there is one choreographer who is to blame for the caesura between dance that expresses beauty or emotion and dance that refers solely to itself, it is Koert Stuyf. Some people call his *Mutation* dance's death blow, while others see it as the overture to something completely new. This happening opened at *Het Nationale Ballet* (HNB), whose director walked out of the performance but had already provided the opportunity for the experiment.

Openness and innovation appear to be essential characteristics of Dutch dance, even in the established circuit. Despite this, in the mid-sixties modern dance emerged on the margins, a separate genre with as many styles as creators. The diversity of both circuits makes dance in the Netherlands look full of life. This is why its history has to be written on the basis of this division between the established circuit and modern dance. In this introduction the names of individual dancers will not be mentioned, but this will be compensated for in the portraits.

Halfway through the last century the development of dance went into overdrive. The standard of performance improved substantially and ballet was given a modern face. It was on these foundations that young choreographers matured and even developed into leading international artists. In the sixties, Hans van Manen set a trend with his *Danstheater*. The seventies were golden years for *Het Nationale Ballet*, with Rudi van Dantzig, Van Manen and Toer van Schayk. In the last quarter of the century, Jiří Kylián brought fame to the *Nederlands Dans Theater* (NDT). On the other hand, these modern dance choreographers are not trendsetters. They imitate art, especially that of New York. Only recently has this sector drawn international acclaim, notable names being Leine & Roebana, Emio Greco & PC Scholten and Ed Wubbe's *Scapino Ballet Rotterdam*.

Dance Comes from Abroad

The art of dance does not develop by way of academies or other institutions. Most learning is by experience. The course of this development is determined by individuals: choreographers and heads of companies with their artistic insight, ballet masters and teachers with their professional skills. Often they come from outside the Netherlands. In fact in its early stages theatrical dance was entirely imported. The Stadtholders of the House of Orange imitated the French court with allegorical courtly ballets. In the early nineteenth century French ballet masters taught romantic ballets to companies in The Hague and Amsterdam. Substantial areas of the country were under the influence of the clergy and dance was considered sinful. Culture was dominated by Calvinism and conservatism. It is not surprising that in 1905, after a tour of the Netherlands and having given birth to her daughter there, the revolutionary Isadora Duncan chose Paris as her base. One or two people in the Netherlands imitated her dancing but this trail is very hard to trace. Anna Pavlova was no more influential. This ballerina died in The Hague in 1929, which made more of an impression than the performances by *Les Ballets Russes* a few years earlier.

Attempts made in the thirties to get classical ballet up and running led to nothing. Nor did the modernism represented by Mondrian and Rietveld have any counterpart in dance. That would have needed a progressive institution like the *Bauhaus*, where experiments were carried out in dance as a kinetic art. Modern

Koert Stuyf's *Mutation*, Het Nationale Ballet, 1967
(Photo Maria Austria / MAI)

Ellen Edinoff in Koert Stuyf's *Seesaw*,
Stichting Eigentijdse dans, 1973 (Photo Maria Austria / MAI)

expressionist dance did catch on in progressive, intellectual artistic circles, however. Female dancers went to Germany, because that was where the great figures of the *Ausdrucktanz* performed: Rudolf Laban, Mary Wigman, Harald Kreuzberg and Yvonne Georgi. Georgi settled in Amsterdam, where, before and during the German occupation, she helped lay the foundations for a generation of dancers who were only free to develop fully after 1945. They did not want to dance in the 'German' style. In the years of reconstruction, they turned to the ballet of Paris, London and New York.

A variety of groups formed in The Hague and Amsterdam. Such 'founding mothers' as Nel Roos, Hans Snoek and the Russian Sonia Gaskell played an important part in this; the same applies, slightly later, to the American Benjamin Harkarvy. The ballet director Sonia Gaskell adopted Diaghilev's motto of creating room for innovation. She and the French ballet director Françoise Adret presented modern work by Béjart and the neoclassicist Balanchine. The romantic classical repertoire was danced too, or at least parts or individual acts from it. The *Holland Festival* programmed the *New York City Ballet* and the *American Ballet Theatre* and French and English ballet stars. The virtuosity of the Russians could be seen on the cinema screen. Rudi van Dantzig was greatly impressed by Ulanova's expressive performance of *Julia*. Hans van Manen preferred American swing and studied Fred Astaire's tap dancing. These two choreographers were the parameters within which ballet developed between 1960 and 1990: the former was an inspired man who translated ideals and failure into modern ballet in an expressionist style, while the latter was a temperamental worldly man who gave his neoclassical ballet contemporary appeal.

Both made their debuts in the mid-fifties. Modern American dance had by then penetrated into Europe. Martha Graham's performance in Amsterdam in 1954 made a powerful impression. Her expressionist style was captivating for its *contraction and release* technique, by which intense emotions are expressed. Her idiom turned out to be as relentlessly angular as Picasso's Cubism, and the psychological themes, influenced by Freud and Jung, were new. The *Nederlands Dans Theater* and *Het Nationale Ballet* invited choreographers from her school to work with them. Anna Solokov and Pearl Lang made reference to such intellectual concepts as alienation, solitude and nonconformism. These were topics that reflected the dark mood of postwar life.

For one or two choreographers the intellectual substance of modern ballet was provided by a sour existentialism and morbid absurdism derived from Beckett and Kafka. Jaap Flier's *Het proces* (The Trial, 1955) is a striking example of this, as is Van Dantzig's debut, *Nachteiland* (Night Island, 1955). He has the dancers perform on their *pointes* but depicts the leading character's inner struggle in a modern, symbolic way. The theme - choosing between harmonious happiness and the pursuit of an ideal - already exposes the rebellious romantic he later turned out to be. Van Dantzig's themes are the transience of life, love, parting and death - 'suffering' as his biographer Luuk Utrecht put it - which were developed to the full in his lyrical *Vier Letzte Lieder* (1977). The socially-critical ballets of the eighties were painful and sarcastic and were so much bound to the spirit of the age that they later almost vanished from the repertoire. Van Dantzig proved his talents even more as the inspiring head of *Het Nationale Ballet* (1968-1991). He was an innovator but turned out to be primarily a creditable keeper of the romantic tradition, which he also enriched with clever versions of *Romeo and Juliet* and *Swan Lake*.

A Dutch 'School'?
Graham's searching work did not appeal at all to Hans van Manen. He drew his inspiration from jazz, to which he set tightly-structured dancing. His great examples were Jerome Robbins and Balanchine. As the choreographer and leader of the *Nederlands Dans Theater*, founded in 1959, he flirted with conceptual dance (*Ready*

Rudi van Dantzig's *Nachteiland* (Night Iland), Het Nationale Ballet, 1955
(Photo G. van Leeuwen / TIN)

Made) and asked contemporary artists to design for his works. His preference for neoconstructivist art took shape in the austere, mathematical, tube-lit sets by Jean-Paul Vroom. They gave his ballet a modern feel. His dance was typified by simplicity and clarity, for which reason he was called 'the Mondrian of dance' and 'master of simplicity'. Like Balanchine's work, his musically inspired ballets appear abstract. Nevertheless, apart from dealing with dance itself, they are about relationships (sometimes of power) between people, and about emotions, though this lies below the surface. The austerity of the dance *idiom* acts as a neutralising coat of varnish over a figuration that arises out of a passionate temperament. Form and content balance each other so well that neither aestheticism nor sentiment or pathos is given a chance.

A striking example of this lucid style is *Grosse Fuge* (1969). His experimental duet *Twylight* (1974) marks his transition to *Het Nationale Ballet*, whose resident choreographer he was from 1974 to 1986. This group's more classical approach inspired him to create *Adagio Hammerklavier* (1974). In that ballet he concisely summarised Beethoven's mature piano music and emotional profundity, with the closing duet, decelerated to the extreme, as the climax of the portrayal of the ecstasy of love. After he returned to the *Nederlands Dans Theater*, led by Kylián, in 1988, he created small-scale works such as the duets *Andante* and *Two*. While there, he worked with dancers who employed the academic technique with no balletic articulation or aesthetics. This gave his late work a strikingly gentle character. Recently, Van Manen has again accentuated pure virtuosity, as in *Solo*. In 2000, as a link between the two major companies, he was awarded the prestigious Erasmus Prize. The part he has played in Dutch dance is comparable to that of Béjart in France and Belgium.

If there were such a thing as a Dutch 'school', Toer van Schayk would also be a member alongside Van Dantzig and Van Manen. It was only in 1972, after a dance career at *Het Nationale Ballet*, that he started as a choreographer. His work is dramatic, like that of Van Dantzig. However, his idiom is rugged and sculptural in line. His work - including the cycles entitled *Pyrrhische Dansen* (Pyrrhic Dances, 1974-1991) and *Sonnetten aan een broer* (Sonnets to a Brother, 1994-1998) - was often sombre and ominous. It was created by someone caught between frightening memories of war and menacing images of the future. Yet his work can also be poetic and even humorous. Van Schayk is also an exceptional designer, both for his own work and that of Van Dantzig. In the frequently reflective set and costume designs one can discern the sculptor which he originally was, especially in their spatiality and tasteful colours. The peak of playful inventiveness was *Notenkraker en Muizenkoning* (Nutcracker and Mouse-King, 1998) which he made with Wayne Eagling.

The work of these three is too varied to be called a Dutch 'school'. The one thing they do have in common is that they have remained faithful to ballet technique. This is not the only respect in which Jiří Kylián differs from them. This Czech choreographer came to work at the *Nederlands Dans Theater* in 1973 and provided the group with a powerful rejuvenating impulse. As its leader, he transformed the NDT into a contemporary group that has been able to display its brilliant and expressive modern style all over the world. Since *Sinfonietta*, he has been acclaimed as a 'European wonderboy', especially in the United States. In 1978 he became its one and only artistic director. In addition to being its choreographer he is also the architect of what is now a three-part company - in addition to the core group there is the youth group (NDT2) and the project with older performers (NDT3). In 1999 he gave up his position at its head. He has had a great influence on international dance, comparable to that of his contemporary William Forsythe. This cosmopolitan - who risks his life on a bicycle in the traffic of The Hague - is a real treasure to the Netherlands: an artist of international reputation who transcends the Dutch borders.

Monique Sand, Alexandra Radius, Han Ebbelaar, Sonja Marchiolli
and Francis Sinceretti (left to right) and Henny Jurriëns (invisible)
in Hans van Manen's *Adagio Hammerklavier*, Het Nationale Ballet, 1973
(Photo J. Fatauros / TIN)

Coleen Davis in Hans van Manen's *Live,*
Het Nationale Ballet, 1979 (Photo J. Fatauros / TIN)

1960 to 1970: Exciting Years

The sixties brought a complete change of mentality, with feminists and students undermining authority. Magical Amsterdam was a place for experimentation with sex and drugs. The contrary spirit of the times was reflected in the established ballet scene. Van Dantzig's *Monument voor een gestorven jongen* (Monument for a Dead Boy, 1965) was about burgeoning homosexual feelings, while in *Life* (1979), the monarchy was criticised and the dancers sang the *Internationale*. *Mutations* (Van Manen / Tetley, 1969) featured naked dancers, though only on film. But Koert Stuyf, an artist who continued to see dance as a visual art, after a study of ballet and modern dance, was even more radical because of his conceptual approach. In 1964 he founded the *Stichting Eigentijdse Dans* (Contemporary Dance Foundation) with the American dancer Ellen Edinoff, who had been trained 'Graham-Style'. They initially created performances in the vein of *Fluxus*, not involving the expression of feelings but simply separate actions: impersonal notions such as space and time and the essence of movement. His postmodern dance was composed of everyday movements. This duo took part in anarchistic art events. In *Verend Trottoir* (Sprung Pavement, in Amsterdam's *Stedelijk Museum*, 1970) passers-by became 'dancers' because the pavement had been covered with rubber tiles. This was followed, between 1970 and 1974, by the events at the *Carré* theatre in Amsterdam, performances in which Edinoff was the magnetic focus. Influenced by Zen Buddhism, Stuyf replaced his conceptualism by contemplation. In *Seesaw* (1973), Edinoff strutted like a geisha along a plank balanced over a barrel like a seesaw. It was enchanting for both its tension and its beauty. *Calico* (1974) presented Japanese-style stillness: dance stripped of all ornament. Satie's serene piano music intensified the expression of this minimal dance. The duo themselves then disappeared from the stage, but not without leaving successors. After a career with his brother, Bart Stuyf became fascinated by Robert Wilson's visual theatre in the United States. From 1969, with *Multi Media*, he created performances at special locations. His highly visual acts involving movement - using objects he had made himself - had a poetic eloquence. His later work, *Spiegels* (Mirrors, 1978), in which he examined dance by means of observation, was more analytical, as was *Target* (1985) in which he brought dance face to face with robotic techniques. Krisztina de Châtel and Truus Bronkhorst also followed in the footsteps of Koert Stuyf. The former took up Stuyf's minimalism and the latter used Edinoff's performance art as a point of departure. Both became leading creative artists who still dominate dance today.

At the same time as Stuyf, Pauline de Groot was also influenced by modern and postmodern American dance. She derived her style, based on *release,* from Erick Hawkins and, later, improvisation from Steve Paxton. Her pieces *Regenmakers* (Rain-Makers, 1968) and *Stap Stenen* (Stepping Stones, 1979) are linked to nature by way of eastern inspiration. The studio set up by this pioneer of modern dance formed the basis of the present *School voor Nieuwe Dans Ontwikkelingen* (SDNO, School of New Developments in Dance) in Amsterdam, which is now linked to the international movement of *contact and improv dance*.

In the sixties, a substantial number of dancers discovered anti-psychological modern dance in America. Merce Cunningham was to the moderns what Balanchine had been to the creators of ballet. These dancers included Ton Lutgerink, Ton Simons, Bianca van Dillen, Pauline Daniëls and Käthy Gosschalk. Alongside Amsterdam and The Hague, Rotterdam too grew into a city of contemporary culture where architecture, design and dance flourished. In New York, Van Dillen was fascinated by Cunningham's concept of chance and Cage's philosophy of linking art directly to life. Her women's collective, *Dansproductie*, created *Lopen* (Walking, 1979). Five women dancers walk through the town immediately before the performance: everyday matters provide the building blocks for the dance. In the same year, Van Manen presented a memorable evening, also in *Carré*: in his video-ballet,

Bart Stuyf's *Spiegels*, Multi Media, 1978
(Photo B. van Dantzig / TIN)

Pauline Daniëls, Margie Smit, Truus Bronkhorst and Patricia Kennedy
(left to right) and Bianca van Dillen (lying) in *Lopen* (Walking),
Stichting Dansproductie, 1979 (Photo B. van Dantzig / TIN)

called *Live*, the audience sees the soloist on a screen as she leaves the theatre at the end of the performance and walks away along the Amstel. *Live* was a dramatic ballet about saying goodbye, while *Lopen* was a prosaic manifesto of anti-illusory dance. The sharp caesura that Stuyf brought about in 1967 also applies here, between emotionally-charged ballet and the modern and postmodern dance that refers only to itself.

A Face of its Own

In the eighties, modern dance was driven mainly by women. A few followed the neutral tone set by the postmodernists, but their work was more often emotionally tinted, as in Käthy Gosschalk's *Nailed* (1984), an abstract dramatic work about the battle of the sexes. The absurd dance theatre of Lisa Marcus and Barbara Duyfjes was all about female sensuality. Their trilogy *Available Angels* (1986-1988) had an autobiographical slant. Self-portraits in the form of solos came into vogue. The ones by Truus Bronkhorst were full of tragedy and irony. In *Portrait* (1983), Van Manen emphasised Pauline Daniëls' androgynous appearance. Arnold Goores - a man amongst women - revealed desires in a moving and witty piece called *Een enkele reis naar zee* (A One-Way Ticket to the Sea, 1985). Désirée Delauney displayed her body as a metaphor for her vulnerable soul in an intimate piece called *Alcool* (Alcohol, 1993). This was 'meaningful dance', but without the harping tone that characterises the corresponding literary genre. These are, rather, powerful portraits of highly individual artists who elevate personal experience to a universal level and make dance into theatre that is both fascinating and entertaining.

Not all work by women had this personal tint. Van Dillen fell under the spell of impersonal minimalism. Jacqueline Knoops made pure dance. Music originating from the modern classics or modern jazz added a lively element to some work, including that of Beppie Blankert. Others looked to words. 'Literary choreography' was the term Gale used to describe the work she made with the director Mark Timmers and the choreographer Lutgerink, based on the writings of Gertrude Stein and Margaret Atwood. Gale and Lutgerink's fragmentary acting-dance style was light and playful. Lutgerink and Van Dillen's *Mariënbad* (1984) was a true milestone in this postmodern 'collection of image and words'. Words, images and movement were linked associatively and edited together loosely like scenes in a film: the whole thing was as diffuse as the ideas, scraps of fictional recollection from Alain Robbe-Grillet's *ciné-roman*, on which it was based. The trilogy *Private & Public Acts* by *Cloud Chamber* (Ron Bunzl, Désirée Delauney, Boris Gerrets and José-Louis Greco) was similar in its many layers and its multidisciplinary approach. Gerrets' *The Twilight Club* (1988) was about 'stardom' and the exposure of the feelings connected to it (suffering, pain, pleasure). Its setting in a forbidden decadent club made it a Pop Art version of Plato's cave story. Bunzl also brought high and low culture together in *Mise-en-cadre* (1989) in which he juggled with appearance and reality as if on a film set. This also showed his love of vaudeville and circus. *Mariënbad* and the collective *Cloud Chamber* signalled the arrival of a new sort of postmodernism that was related to the literary, philosophical movement. This postmodernism gave colour to the dance by its use of 'narrative' but fragmented structures, 'characters' and eclecticism of design, music and dance idiom.

The nineties saw the dawn of some lean years after this explosively colourful era. The new generation made its appearance only cautiously and piecemeal, unlike elsewhere in Europe. The Netherlands' initial headstart now turned to its disadvantage. The moderns were now mature forty-year-olds and continued on their own course, without producing any radically new or different work. What was new in the nineties was a renewed interest in the development of a dance idiom: one based on the mechanics of the physique and always drawing on personal ideas and feelings. Like a rather indefinable linkage of body and mind. Forsythe's *nine-point system*

Nicki Wentholt and Daniël Niemann in Ton Lutgerink and Bianca van Dillen's, *Mariënbad*, Stichting Dansproductie and Studio's Onafhankelijk Toneel, 1984 (Photo J. Linders / TIN)

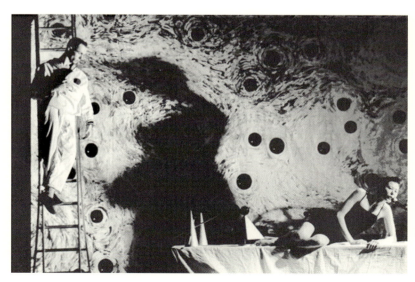

Paul Selwyn Norton and Kirsten de Groot in Boris Gerrets' *The Twilight Club*, Cloud Chamber, 1988 (Photo M. Boyer)

and improvisation became accepted training methods, combined with lessons in classical technique. The modern dance taboo regarding virtuosity was abandoned. The fragmentary, organic style this yielded was introduced by a group of freelance dancers / co-creators and choreographers. The stylistic differences between Anouk van Dijk, Bruno Listopad, Paul Selwyn Norton and (Diane) Elshout & (Frank) Händeler were fairly minimal. A few stood out amidst this uniformity and gave their own personal content to this new dance: Leine & Roebana, Emio Greco and Nanine Linning.

Modern dance in the Netherlands took on an appearance of its own. The influence of Cunningham and the American postmoderns, virtually all of whom performed there, was limited to the imitation of methods and approaches. Even a Cunningham adept like Ton Simons eventually made his work very much his own. And of course Pina Bausch's dance-theatre was a great influence, as was Anne Teresa de Keersmaeker's *Rosas*. In the shape of Jan Fabre's mythical ballets, Marc Vanrunxt's symbolism, Wim Vandekeybus' theatrical dance, Alain Platel's raw dance-theatre and Meg Stuart's physical theatre, this 'Flemish' dance was and still is a powerful presence in the Netherlands. The epigones turned out to last only a very short time. Rather, the performances from abroad provided a welcome supplement to domestic offerings. Audiences want a bit of everything and are just as open to Japanese *butoh* as to French hiphop. Diversity and openness. In this respect little has changed over all these centuries.

BIBLIOGRAPHY

EVA VAN SCHAIK, *Op gespannen voet. Geschiedenis van de Nederlandse theaterdans*, Uitgeverij De Haan / Unieboek, Haarlem / Bussum, 1981.

MONIEK MERKX, *Studio's Onafhankelijk Toneel*, Rotterdam, 1985.

JOCHEN SCHMIDT, *Der Zeitgenosse als Klassiker. Über den holländischen Choreographen Hans van Manen*, Ballett-Bühnen-Verlag / Kallmeyer, Cologne, 1987.

LUUK UTRECHT, *Het Nationale Ballet 25 jaar. De geschiedenis van Het Nationale Ballet van 1961 tot 1986*, Uitgeverij Allert de Lange and Het Nationale Ballet, Amsterdam, 1987.

COOS VERSTEEG, *Nederlands Dans Theater. Een revolutionaire geschiedenis*, Uitgeverij Balans, Amsterdam, 1987.

LUUK UTRECHT, *Rudi van Dantzig, een omstreden idealist in het ballet*, Walburg Pers, Zutphen, 1991.

ARIEJAN KORTEWEG, 'Les Pays-Bas, plateau tournant de la danse', in *Septentrion, revue de culture néerlandaise*, XXIII, 1994, no. 1, pp. 43-48.

ISABELLA LANZ, *Een tuin met duizend bloemen – Jiří Kylián 20 jaar Nederlands Dans Theater*, Theater Instituut Nederland, Amsterdam, 1995.

ISABELLA LANZ, A *Garden of Dance, Jiří Kylián 20 Years at Nederlands Dans Theater,* Theater Instituut Nederland, Amsterdam, 1995.

EVA VAN SCHAIK, *Hans van Manen. Leven & Werk*, Uitgeverij Arena, Amsterdam, 1997.

International Encyclopedia of Dance, Oxford University Press, New York / Oxford, 1998 (vol. 4: 'Netherlands' and 'Manen, Hans van'; vol. 2: 'Dantzig, Rudi van').

ISABELLA LANZ and MARCEL-ARMAND VAN NIEUWPOORT (eds.), *Toer van Schayk. Drie dimensies in Dans*, Uitgeverij Walburg Pers, Zutphen, 1998.

GER VAN LEEUWEN and MAARTJE WILDEMAN (eds.), *Dansfotografie in Nederland – Dance Photography in the Netherlands*, International Theater Film Books, Amsterdam, 1998.

ANNA AALTEN and MIRJAM VAN DER LINDEN, 'The Dutch Don't Dance', in *Europe Dancing. Perspectives on Theatre, Dance and Cultural Identity*. Routledge, London, 2000.

COOS VERSTEEG (ed.), *Dancing Dutch. Contemporary Dance in the Netherlands*, Theater Instituut Nederland, Amsterdam, 2000.

www.tin.nl
www.dansbeweegtje.nl

Krisztina de Châtel

A powerful fist, concentrated tension in a compact form. This image is evocative of the work of Krisztina de Châtel, from *Lines* in 1979 to *Rooms* in 2002. The essence of her work has not changed with time, each piece being rather a variation on a theme. Yet the colour of her work changes, partly through the efforts of the artists with whom she always looks to collaborate. By linking up with contemporary art (Minimal and Conceptual Art in the eighties, video and computer art more recently) her work grows in parallel with the times. One constant is her neutral *minimal dance* idiom that is chameleon-like in its ability to fit perfectly into this, while conversely also possessing a compelling force by which the art is absorbed into the whole.

De Châtel initially sought contact with artists working with light (fluorescent) and energy. For *Lines*, Jan van Munster designed a square 'cage' of fluorescent tubes. They are covered with black on the outside, so that the light 'forces' its way through a crack, representing emotional tension. De Châtel has five women dancers perform restrained phrases of movement in this closed light-cage: a series of fast basic classical steps that divide the space into geometric patterns and manipulate time by means of deceleration and acceleration. The dance is in step with the repetitive structure of Philip Glass' minimal *Music with Changing Parts*. *Lines* contained the germ of many of De Châtel's later *leitmotifs*: the struggle between openness and restriction, freedom and bondage, and also between form and content and abstraction and meaning.

After a series of aesthetic choreographic pieces of *minimal dance*, to which *Change* (partly designed by Peter Struycken) belongs, her dances became more dynamic. The conceptual artists Conrad van de Ven and Peter Vermeulen urged her to let her dance enter into dialogue with their designs. They devise barriers against which the dancers struggle: a circular earthen rampart (*Föld*) against which the dancers slogged away and a hurricane (*Typhoon*) against which they competed. In *Staunch* the dancers got stuck between partitions that slammed shut. These trials of physical and mental strength were conceived as an existential struggle: as fought by the choreographer, of course. De Châtel's dance became more dramatic when she started working with Niek Kortekaas, a set designer. *Dualis* was a surprising turning point in which she conveyed feelings of uncertainty and solitude in a theatrical way. After that, themes such as power and jealousy (*Imperium*), love and loneliness (*Weep, Cry and Tangle*) and transience and death (*Vanitas*) appeared more often in her choreography, backed up by stage sets with an often unmistakable symbolism. It was only in *Paletta* that she again moulded intense feelings - of isolation - into an abstract form, by putting women dancers in transparent cylinders.

In the nineties she expanded on her dance themes by using outdoor locations, films and interactive dance with video and computer. The theme of 'struggle' is portrayed in her film *Blindside Block*, in which dancers battle against a team of sturdy American football players. In *Ló*, which was made in the dunes, the dancers do *pas de deux* with performing horses. This archetypal image of man and animal has an enchanting effect in the twilight. *Waterlanders*, created on the island of Terschelling, is about the elements wind, water, earth (sand) and fire (light). The pieces she then devised with the computer artist Quirine Racké were, conversely, far

Photo S. Vanfleteren

removed from nature. In the playful *Lara*, named after the cybergirl Lara Croft in *Tomb Raider*, a real live female dancer takes up the struggle against her virtual *alter ego* on the screen. In *LinkAge*, the Japanese multimedia collective *Nest* bombards the dancers and set with manipulated video images.

This hectic virtual art and a moment of contemplation of the 'traditional' painting of Armando (*Bewogen Bomen* - Moved Trees) was followed by *Objectworx*, a solo for the dancer Cecilia Moisio, which she danced round transparent panels on which her movements were simultaneously captured on video and manipulated, like delicate drawings sketched by hand. *Rooms*, a group work, was quite sophisticated, with a continuous state of dynamic balance created using dance, set, lighting and music.

De Châtel always tries to find a balance between extremes. This quest for equilibrium stems from her being Dutch, but of Hungarian origins: temperamental but with a tendency towards extreme order and control. Like Bartók and Mondrian in one person. By coincidence, she also encountered contradictory views during her training. Expressionism *and* the impersonal *Bauhaus* style in Germany, conceptual dance *and* the Graham technique in Amsterdam. The fact that she was able to forge some kind of unity out of this says something about her intuition as a dancer and

21

ROOMS, 2002

Photo D. van Meer

her intelligence as a creative artist. She also allows her dancers to develop into individual personalities: Sjoukje Osinga, Josje Neuman, Cathy Dekker, Karin Post, Juliëtte Inger, Ann van den Broek and Suzan Tunca, Oerm Matern, Dries van der Post, Gilles den Hartog and Massimo Molinari, to name a few of the more prominent ones.

KRISZTINA DE CHÂTEL

Budapest (Hungary), b. 1943

EDUCATION AND CAREER

Studied at the *Folkwang Hochschule* in Essen.

First worked as a dancer with *Stichting Eigentijdse Dans* and as a dancer and actress with *BEWTH* .
Founded the *Dansgroep Krisztina de Châtel* in 1976.
Made her choreographic debut in 1977 (*Voltage Control I*).

WORKS

Voltage Control I (1977), *Lines*, 1979; *Light*, 1980; *Forgo*, 1982; *Thron*, 1984; *Solos I, II, III*, 1985; *Föld*, 1985; Typhoon, 1986; *Staunch*, 1987; *Change*, 1988; *Dualis*, 1989; Imperium, 1990; *Paletta*, 1992; Weep, Cry and Tangle, 1992; *Facetten,* 1994; *Muralis*, 1994; *Solo IV* , 1995; *Vanitas*, 1996; *Ló*, 1997; *Lara*, 1998; *Solo VI*, 1999; *Epoxy*, 1999; *Lara and Friends*, 1999; *LinkAge*, 2000; *Dynamix*, 2000; *Objectworx*, 2001; *Waterlanders*, 2001; *Rooms*, 2002; *Slag*, 2002 (for *Het Nationale Ballet*)

BIBLIOGRAPHY

Eva van Schaik, 'Krisztina de Châtel. Balanceren tussen bekken en brein', in *Ons Erfdeel*, XXXIII, 1990, no. 1, pp. 24-30.
Eva van Schaik, 'Krisztina de Châtel, navette entre extrêmes', in *Septentrion, revue de culture néerlandaise*, XX, 1991, no. 4, pp. 41-46.
'Krisztina de Châtel', in *Dancing Dutch. Contemporary Dance in the Netherland*s, Theater Instituut Nederland, Amsterdam, 2000.
Jacqueline Algra (ed.), *Krisztina de Châtel - Dwars door de ruimte* (articles by Isabella Lanz and Mirjam van der Linden), Amsterdam, 2001 (in Dutch and English).
'25 jaar Krisztina de Châtel', in *TM* , special issue, December 2001 - January 2002.

FILMS - VIDEOS - TELEVISION RECORDINGS

Staunch, NOS, 1990; *Dansgroep Krisztina de Châtel*, NOS, 1991; *Paletta*, NPS, 1993; *Stalen Neuzen*, NPS / BRTN, 1996; *Blindside Block* (in collaboration with The American Crusadors), 1998

ADDRESS

Dansgroep Krisztina de Châtel, Luchtvaartstraat 2, NL-1059 CA Amsterdam
Tel.: +31 (0)20 6 695 755
Fax: +31 (0)20 6 696 864
info@dechatel.nl
www.dechatel.nl

Truus Bronkhorst once called herself a 'dancer by origin and with passion'. This was no exaggeration, because she is totally devoted to dance and all her work derives from her emotions. She has now been describing feelings and thoughts with grand gestures and serene dance steps for twenty years. She continues in the tradition of the great modern dance expressionists in her own contemporary way, and it has to be said that she started at a time, in the heyday of postmodern dance, when expressionism was taboo in dance. She immediately showed that she was very much at home with rebellion and individuality. This image as a dance nonconformist fits her no less now.

It was early on that Bronkhorst came into contact with a form of modern dance that appealed to her. She learnt from Koert Stuyf how to seek the essence in movement, and from Edinoff the magic of performance. It was then at *Dansproductie* that she learnt the crafts of dancing and choreography. In the early eighties she operated in squatters' art circles and the underground nightlife that Joost Zwagerman described in his novel *Gimmick*. She swapped her contrary performances for appearances at the Shaffy Theatre. The director Rob Malasch pointed her in the direction of solo performances. She created an outstanding series of them herself: after *Truus Bronkhorst danst Truus Bronkhorst*, she made her breakthrough with *Lood*, followed by *Goud* and *Bloed* (Lead, Gold & Blood). In these pieces she appeared as mysterious mystic and oriental geisha, queen and heroine, whore, knight and jester. She used simple props that became a permanent ingredient of her visual language: a black balloon as a symbol of the weight of existence, which nevertheless defies gravity, a gun as an instrument of machismo, peacock feathers for the art of female seduction, a mirror as a ballet prop and symbol of introspection. Together with these symbols there were the colours black, red and white and the poses of Christ on the Cross, the descent from the Cross and the Pietà.

These solos were about love, suffering, unfulfilled desires, solitude and death. And although these themes were created explicitly on the basis of her own female view, she was able to raise them to a universal level. In her vital and deadly serious questions she only just avoided pathos, but was able to rein it in with irony: she allowed space for humour alongside deep emotion. The grand melodramatic gesture and provocation became her trade marks.

Her strength lay originally in her own performances. Their intensity enabled her to draw the audience along with her. The restrained classical dance movements - repetitive and clearly marked - also gave her work an aura of pure beauty. To this was added rigid timing with digitally precise transitions. Her choreographic talents were expressed more clearly in her group pieces, in which Marien Jongewaard was increasingly involved. His influence was already evident in *Zwarte bloesem* (Black Blossom), in which the then thirty-year-old dancer surrounded herself with three young black men. With this trio she danced a bold game of black versus white, old versus young, woman versus man. The sexual undertone was subtle, while the political comment, with the bluster of Mussolini and Archie Shepp's jazz pamphlet *Mama Rose*, was explicit. This protest against the inequality of men and women, rich and poor, black and white, and against the superficiality and superiority of Western society played an even more important part in the group pieces she made later, with

Photo S. Vanfleteren

Jongewaard as co-creator and dramaturge. *Wonderful World*, *Goodbye Body* and *Truus Bronkhorst, Marien Jongewaard... and Friends* were cynical in tone and raw in form. They were confrontational, as a result of their emphasis on the physical violence between men, as for example expressed in the duet of hitting and hitting back by Jean-Louis Barning and Jakob Nissen. Looking back, this trilogy, together with the all-male piece *1, 2, 1, 2, 3, 4*, formed the transition to *THE FALL*, *Soul* and *Mongoolse dansen* (Mongolian Dances).

In these last group pieces Bronkhorst and Jongewaard rediscovered the balance between beauty and drama. They zoomed in on male behaviour, with all its bravura, vulnerability, vanity and tenderness, in which a touch of homo-eroticism also played a part. They equally reflected their rage about the world's troublespots. They contained a remarkably large proportion of pure dance. The longer passages drew their strength from the repetition of very meticulous patterns and formations of movement whose classical lucidity was reminiscent of Hans van Manen.

Simplicity of design remained an essential characteristic of all her work, as did the thematically selected music. In the latter case she displayed from the very beginning the taste of a true eclectic: choosing music by the *chansonnier* Jacques Brel and the soul queen Nina Simone, by the medieval Hildegard von Bingen and the

MONGOOLSE DANSEN
(Mongolian Dances),

2001

Photo L. van Velzen

experimental Olga Gubaidolina, by the avant-garde rock musician Jimi Hendrix and his postmodern successor Prince, by Arvo Pärt and Erik Satie and even Mozart's entire *Requiem*, in each case setting the right tone for her dance.

Truus Bronkhorst no longer dances herself, but she has succeeded in transferring her expressive and yet succinct idiom, surprisingly enough, to men, including not only the masculine Barning and Nissen but also the feminine Marc van Loon. Three black dancers, the powerful Ian Butler, the slight Percy Kruythoff and the muscled Jacques Laurant Madiba have recently given a dark import to this expressiveness.

TRUUS BRONKHORST

Heerlen, b. 1951

EDUCATION AND CAREER

Studied at the *Dansacademie Nel Roos* in Rotterdam and the *Theaterschool Amsterdam* (modern dance department).

Also studied psychology in Amsterdam.

Made her choreographic debut in 1979 (*Circuit 3*).

Cofounder of and dancer and choreographer with *Stichting Dansproductie*, *Vals bloed*, and the *Nationaal Fonds*.

In 1986 founded the *Stichting van de Toekomst* (advised by Marien Jongewaard).

WORKS

Circuit 3, 1979; *Truus Bronkhorst in concert*, 1986; *Truus Bronkhorst danst Truus Bronkhorst*, 1987; *Lood*, 1988; *Goud*, 1989; *Branco*, 1990; *Zwarte bloesem*, 1990; *Bloed*, 1992; *Wonderful World*, 1995; *Goodbye Body*, 1995; *Truus Bronkhorst, Marien Jongewaard ... and Friends*, 1997; *THE FALL* 1997; *Tryptich*, 1998; *1, 2, 1, 2, 3, 4*, 1999; *Soul*, 2000; *Mongoolse dansen*, 2001

BIBLIOGRAPHY

Frénk van der Linden, 'Ik vind het publiek een verwend huilerig kind', in *De Tijd*, 6 February 1987.

Isabella Lanz, 'Truus Bronkhorst', in *Binnenstebuiten - Vrouwen en moderne dans in Nederland*, exhib. cat., Amsterdam, 1990.

Isabella Lanz, 'Truus Bronkhorst: ik relativeer niet meer', in *Notes*, 4 April 1990.

Ariejan Korteweg, 'Tovenaar en tovenaarsleerling', in *de Volkskrant*, 23 November 1990.

Eva van Schaik, 'Truus Bronkhorst, une danseuse universelle', in *Septentrion, revue de culture néerlandaise*, XXX, 1991, no. 2, pp. 32-36.

Eva van Schaik, 'Bronkhorst en Jongewaard, Julia en Romeo', in *Notes*, January 1994.

Heleen Elfferich, 'Bronkhorst en Jongewaard, Tegendraads', in *Notes*, February 1995.

Annette Embrechts, 'Kinderen uit het paradijs', in *de Volkskrant*, 4 June 1999.

Eva van Schaik, 'Truus Bronkhorst', in *Dancing Dutch. Contemporary Dance in the Netherlands*, Theater Instituut Nederland, Amsterdam, 2000.

FILMS - VIDEOS - TELEVISION RECORDINGS

About Truus Bronkhorst, NOS, 1992; *THE FALL*, NPS, 1998; *Mongoolse dansen*, NPS, 2002

ADDRESS

Stichting van de Toekomst, Plantage Muidergracht 155, NL-1018 TT Amsterdam

Tel.: +31 (0)20 6 934 551

Fax: +31 (0)20 4 636 729

betty.kaan@inter.nl.net

www.truus-bronkhorst.com

Jiří Kylián

Jiří Kylián grew up in postwar Prague, which under the communist regime was sombre and grey. The one ray of light was the conservatory, where he was taught classical ballet, jazz dance and music. He later studied in London, escaped across the Czech border - just before it was closed in 1968 - and was able to join Cranko's *Stuttgart Ballett* as a dancer and choreographer. He joined a tradition of expressionists, confident that he would adapt it to suit himself. 'Motion is emotion' was also an important concept. Occasionally these feelings were of a personal nature, such as his impotence regarding the political destiny of his native country (*Stoolgame*) and in his optimistic ode to freedom, *Sinfonietta* (Jánaček), but they were more often about love, desire, passion, eroticism and death.

Kylián felt akin to such expressionist painters as Edward Munch and to the late romantic composers. His *La Cathédrale engloutie* (Debussy), *Transfigured Night* (Schoenberg), *Songs of a Wayfarer* (Mahler), *Wiegelied* (Berg) and *Symphony of Psalms* (Stravinsky), made with the *Nederlands Dans Theater* between 1975 and 1984, have unbridled energy in addition to their enormous musicality. Their compelling language is worldly and heavenly at the same time. He seamlessly links classical technique to a modern, supple torso and the elasticity found in bare feet. Loosely draped costumes accentuate the dynamics and the continuity in whirling patterns of movement. The dance suggests openness and freedom, even though it expresses psychological conflicts. Kylián paints with verve in a colourful language with broad appeal.

In the mid-eighties he made narrative ballets (*L'Histoire du soldat*, *L'Enfant et les sortilèges*) that illustrated his love of the magic of theatre. At that time he was looking for a new idiom. His stay in Australia, where he watched Aboriginal dance ceremonies, provided him with the stimulus for change, although the solo *Silent Cries* for his wife Sabine Kupferberg can be seen as an overture to his series of *Zwart / Wit* (Black / White) ballets too: *No More Play*, *Sarabande*, *Sweet Dreams*, *Falling Angels* and *Petite mort* are small in scale and simply presented, the sets often black, with light as an essential element. The dance idiom is sharp, angular and abrupt. Kylián does not visually illustrate the music from A to Z, but, on the contrary, tries to penetrate to its heart. In ballets set to the music of Anton Webern he accentuates that composer's aphoristic swipes and dissects the complexity of the texture. The Black / White ballets are abstract and evoke a spectrum of diverse moods and feelings: distressing fickleness as against mild melancholy, frightening alienation as against dreamlike surrealism, light sensuality and dark eroticism. He made this notable series for some brilliant dancers, including Fiona Lumnis, Nancy Euverink, Patrick Delcroix, Johan Inger, Ken Ossola, Elke Schepers, Cora Bos-Kroese, Paul Lightfoot, Brigitte Martin and Jorma Elo.

Kylián's identity as a European creator of ballets is combined with such typically Christian notions as benedictions and visitations, which he initially wove into his work. This means his work is permeated with European music, including Bach. The weaknesses and virtues of man provide material for his work. He cannot deal with contemporary materialism and an overly technocratic society. The inhuman frightens him. He is concerned that man is becoming increasingly alienated from nature. It was from this that his fascination for the Aboriginals arose, with their

Photo S. Vanfleteren

awareness of the unity of man and nature. Over the years the inspiration he drew from Europe has faded. He has turned his gaze to the East. In a civilised Japan he experiences the effects of an old culture; in a philosophy and religion bound up with nature - Taoism and Zen Buddhism, in the inventive construction of temples and gardens of meditation and the graceful calligraphy. He is fascinated by the combination of age-old things with what is futuristically new. He met the modern composer Toru Takemitsu as early as the seventies. This Japanese thread runs from *Torso* and *Dream Time* through *Kaguyahime* (Maki Isshi) to the present and is still gaining strength. The atmosphere of his recent work is characterised by Eastern spirituality, while the form has more to do with a modern conceptualism, with perception among other things.

In *One of a Kind* many of these apparently contradictory elements come together. The set, by the architect Atsushi Kitagawara, looks like a landscape of ingeniously folded origami, beautiful and unapproachable. There are four solos set to a collage of western and ethnic music. Cora Bos-Kroese opens hers with fitful movements that suit the surroundings, delicate but tough. Kylián's dance idiom makes do with fewer and fewer words, but its great expressiveness remains undiminished. Stepping down from his post as leader of the company allows him to work on special projects.

27'52", 2002
Photo J.-J. Bos

He made *Doux mensonges* for the *Opéra Ballet* in Paris. The labyrinthine interior of the *Opéra Garnier* stimulated his sense of mystery. He introduced the subterranean passages into the ballet using video, with which he often experiments. He did the same in *Blackbird*, a solo for his Japanese muse Megumi Nakamura, which is an ode to sensuality. The group piece *27'52"* displays a new balance between abstract and expressiveness, proven expertise and a sense of experiment, eastern reflections and western existential questions: it is the work of a mature artist who dares to reveal more and more.

JIŘÍ KYLIÁN

Prague (Czech Republic), b. 1947

EDUCATION AND CAREER

Studied at the Conservatory in Prague (under Zora Šemberová) and the *Royal Ballet School* in London.

Leading dancer at the *Stuttgarter Ballet*.
Made his choreographic debut in 1970 (*Paradox*).
Since 1973 has worked at the *Nederlands Dans Theater*, successively as guest choreographer (1973-1975), artistic director & choreographer (1975-1999) and advisor-choreographer (since 1999). Since 2000 has been advisor to the *Saitama Arts Foundation* (Japan).

WORKS

Paradox, 1970; *Stoolgame*, 1974; *La Cathédrale engloutie*, 1975; *Torso*, 1975; *Transfigured Night*, 1975; *Sinfonietta*, 1978; *Symphony of Psalms*, 1978; *Forgotten Land*, 1981; *Symphony in D*, 1981; *Svadebka*, 1982; *Songs of a Wayfarer*, 1982; *Stamping Ground*, 1983; *Wiegelied*, 1983; *Dream Time*, 1983; *L'Enfant et les sortilèges*, 1984; *L'Histoire du soldat, 1986*; *Kaguyahime*, 1988; *No More Play*, 1988; *Falling Angels*, 1989; *Sweet Dreams*, 1990; *Petite mort*, 1991; *Un Ballo*, 1991; *Stepping Stones*, 1991; *No Sleep till Dawn of Day*, 1992; *Double You*, 1994; *Bella Figura*, 1995; *Arcimboldo*, 1995, *Sarabande*, 1995, 2000; *Tears of Laughter*, 1996; *Wings of Wax*, 1997; *One of a Kind*, 1998; *A Way A Lone*, 1998; *Indigo Rose*, 1998; *Half Past*, 1999; *Doux mensonges*, 1999; *Click-Pause-Silence*, 2000; *Blackbird*, 2001; *Claude Pascal*, 2002; *27'52"*, 2002

Kylián's work is on the repertoire of more than 40 companies in Europe, the United States, Canada, Israel and Japan.

BIBLIOGRAPHY

Eva van Schaik, 'Jiří Kylián en het "Nederlands Dans Theater"', in *Ons Erfdeel*, XXXV, 1992, no. 3, pp. 332-342.

Eva van Schaik, 'Jiří Kylián et le 'Nederlands Dans Theater"', in *Septentrion, revue de culture néerlandaise*, XXII, 1993, no. 2, pp. 33-40.

Isabella Lanz, *Een tuin met duizend bloemen – Jiří Kylián 20 jaar Nederlands Dans Theater*, Theater Instituut Nederland, Amsterdam, 1995.

Isabella Lanz, A *Garden of Dance, Jiří Kylián 20 Years at Nederlands Dans Theater*, Theater Instituut Nederland, Amsterdam, 1995.

'Kylián, Jiří', in *International Encyclopedia of Dance*, vol. IV, Oxford University Press, Oxford / New York, 1998, pp. 81-82.

Lesley-Anne Sayers, 'Jiří Kylián', in *Fifty Contemporary Choreographers* (compiled by Martha Bremser), London / New York, 1999, pp. 133-139.

FILMS - VIDEOS - TELEVISION RECORDINGS

Four by Kylián – An Anthology of Modern Ballets Choreographed by Jiří Kylián (*Sinfonietta*, RM Arts / NOS, 1980; *La Cathédrale engloutie*, RM Arts / NOS, 1983; *Torso*, RM Arts / SVT2, 1983; *Svadebka*, RM Arts / NOS, 1984); *A Double Bill of Choreography by Jiří Kylián* (*Symphony in D*, RM ARTS / NOS, 1983; *Stamping Ground*, RM ARTS / NOS, 1987); *Een uur Kylián* (*No More Play*; *Petite mort*; *Falling Angels*), NDT / NOS / RM Arts, 1996; *Bella Figura* (in *Pitch*), NDT / NPS / RM Arts, 1999

ADDRESS

Kylián Foundation, Nobelstraat 1 E, NL-2513 BC Den Haag
Tel.: + 31 (0)70 363 02 08   Fax: + 31 (0)70 363 02 20   kylfound@wxs.nl

Paul Lightfoot

After Nacho Duato, and with Johan Inger, Paul Lightfoot is one of those *Nederlands Dans Theater* dancers who developed into a choreographer under the wing of Jiří Kylián. Lightfoot is still working for this company, which he joined in 1985. He has created an impressive series of ballets, all of whose titles start with the letter 'S'. This comes from the name of his wife Sol León, his colleague, designer and, since 1998, 'official' co-choreographer. When interviewed, Lightfoot says that she is above all his 'third eye', a dance dramaturge who provides him with feedback, shares his thoughts and also helps create the dance.

It is hard to combine choreography with dancing while maintaining a high standard and often being on tour. Much of his work is done under severe pressure. These are not full-length works, but pieces lasting about twenty-five minutes that fit into a *triple bill*. Lightfoot's name is often taken literally. His work is indeed often, but not exclusively,'lightfooted'. He is occasionally requested to provide a certain lightheartedness to counterbalance other, more serious ballets on the bill. This lively aspect usually lies in the whimsicality of unexpected movements, sudden changes of direction, an express forward roll and backward inclination, which makes an exaggerated impression, like an electric eel moving sideways - the impulsive lashing out of legs and arms with flexible joints. It is as if Lightfoot were presenting characters from a comic strip. The men are elastic and monumental, the women elegant and feminine. This is a reflection of Lightfoot and León themselves. In *Sigue* they dance a love duet that is both tender and comical.

Lightfoot's dance is shaped by the modern expressive style of Kylián, but is not a copy of it. The initial emphasis was on entertainment, as in *Shangri-la*, but his image as a playful dance cartoonist gradually changed. It is not that his work became overly serious, rather that it maintains a balance between serious and comical, weighty and self-critical. One of his characteristics is that he links the dance to some unexpected objects. In *So Sorry*, Jeanne Solan dances with a very big humming top, which makes her seem like Alice in Wonderland. These objects are a dominant presence and set the atmosphere. Sometimes they exude a latent threat or create a sense of triviality. In *Solitaire* a man hangs high above the stage in a circus ring in which he can perform all manner of acrobatic feats. Yet the important thing is not his miraculous tumbling but his almost palpable isolation.

In *Said and Done* the image is reversed. The soloist Miguel Oliveira dances directly below a gigantic drum which he repeatedly knocks into by accident and which threatens to crush him. When set against three duets that evoke love, tenderness and solidarity, his being alone becomes tragic. Solitude is equally powerfully depicted in *Speak for Yourself*. Yvan Dubreuil conjures clouds of smoke out of his head and creates a sort of magical *cordon sanitaire* around himself. The others want nothing to do with this odd character. This is both bizarre and distressing. Especially when towards the end the smoke is dispelled by a curtain of water that literally puts all the dancers out in the cold.

Lightfoot is, like Kylián, a true man of the theatre who uses every available means to create the expressive images he has in his mind. The interaction between light and stage setting play a major part in his work, as is the case in *Stilleven* (Still-Life), which is set on a brightly lit carpet of white flour on an otherwise darkened

Photo S. Vanfleteren

stage. His stage settings are often black and white and a grainy grey, as are the photos that Dick Buwalda has taken of rehearsals. He has a striking penchant for early music: Purcell, Bach, Vivaldi and Scarlatti. Here too, Lightfoot juxtaposes light with ponderous, pompous organ music alongside the delicate sounds of a harpsichord. He also likes using old-fashioned popular music and well-worn opera excerpts such as Rossini's overture *La Gazza Ladra*. He opens and closes *Stilleven* with the *Last Post*, played from the back of the auditorium, a desolate sound.

Start to Finish is his first choreography to be significantly more dramatic in tone and clearly made for the dancers: primarily for Lightfoot's temperamental muse Sol León and the dramatic talent of Jorma Elo, whose grotesque gestures he uses to the full. The use of four live drummers who open the piece by marching rigidly in a line across the stage is as absurd as it is compelling. In his more recent pieces he has increasingly made use of the more personal qualities of the dancers with whom he works regularly: in addition to León and Elo, they include Nancy Euverink, Lorraine Blouin, Mário Radacovsky and Stefan Zeromsky.

Safe as Houses combines much of what this duo have already danced, summarising it beautifully. It is enchanting to see the dancers swallowed up and

SAFE AS HOUSES, 2002

Photo D. Buwalda

spat out by a revolving wall in a milk-white stage setting. The way the dancers in pitch-black costumes (León, Elo & Zeromsky) form a block against the individual solo dancers in creamy-white outfits is made dramatic by the contrast. Dreamlike and yet realistic.

PAUL LIGHTFOOT
Kingsley (Great Britain), b. 1966

EDUCATION AND CAREER
Studied at the *Royal Ballet School* in London.

Since 1985 has danced with the *Nederlands Dans Theater* (first NDT2 then NDT1)
Made his choreographic debut in 1989 (*The Bard of Avon*).

WORKS
The Bard of Avon (1989); *Spilt Milk*, 1990; *Step Lightly*, 1991; *Seconds*, 1992; *Sigue*, 1993; *SH-Boom*, 1994; *Softly, as I Leave You*, 1994; *Solitaire*, 1994; *Susto*, 1994; *So Sorry* 1994; *Start to Finish*, 1996; *Skew-whiff*, 1996; *Shangri-la*, 1997; *Stilleven*, 1997; *Singing Apes*, 1998; *Sad Case*, 1998; *Speak for Yourself*, 1999; *Small Moves*, 1999; *Squeaky Wheel*, 2000; *Said and Done*, 2001; *Safe as Houses*, 2002

BIBLIOGRAPHY
Roy van de Graaf, 'Draai het om, dan wordt het iets grappigs', in *de Volkskrant*, 11 April 1997.
Mirjam van der Linden, 'Zelfs stilstaande dansers bewegen' in *NRC Handelsblad*, 4 November 1997.
Mike Dixon, 'Paul Lightfoot – Choreographer', in *Dance Europe*, June - July 1998.

FILMS - VIDEOS - TELEVISION RECORDINGS
Susto, NOS, 1995; *Skew-whiff*, NPS, 1998

ADDRESS
Nederlands Dans Theater, Postbus 333, NL-2501 CH Den Haag
Schedeldoekshaven 60, NL-2511 EN Den Haag
Tel.: +31 (0)70 360 993 1
Fax: +31 (0)70 361 715 6
info@ndt.nl
www.ndt.nl

Ton Simons

To Ton Simons, dance means primarily movement and choreography: moulding bodies in space and time. He sees dance as a visual art. In fact he originally studied to be an artist. This changed at a stroke when he became acquainted with dance at a performance by Merce Cunningham's company. He learnt more about Cunningham's anti-emotional style at the Rotterdam Dance Academy. A grant enabled him to go to the *Cunningham Studio*, where he explored in depth the great man's techniques and theory of chance and autonomy in sound and movement. The influence of Simons' teacher was a marked presence in the first piece he did in Rotterdam. He made use of John Cage's music - according to Cunningham's 'principle of chance' the dancers only hear the music for the first time during the opening performance - and worked in the same way with Michel Waisvisz, an experimental sound composer. After three years he again left for New York, which was then the centre of postmodern dance. Like his contemporaries he used pop music (Dylan, Van Morrison and The Velvet Underground) and worked as a dancer and choreographer on the avant-garde circuit, first with Ellen van Schuylenburch and later with Brenda Daniëls. He saw an opportunity to establish a group. *Ton Simons and Dancers* signalled the start of wild times whose climax came in his performances with live trendsetting bands. *The Palace at 4 A.M.*, *Spinoza Variations* (The Ordinairies) and *Materia prima* (Test Department) were playful pieces: chaotic, hectic and full of noise. Part of the irony lay in their bizarre costumes: the female dancers wore billowing candy-pink tutus with sturdy gym shoes.

Live music is certainly spectacular, but it is demanding. On top of all this, Aids reared its ugly head, particularly in dance circles. The wild days were over. Rage and a mature realisation of mortality penetrated into Simons' work, in such eloquent titles as *Sleepless Nights* and *Black Mirror* and symbolic objects like a cross and a skull. Music, especially that of Mozart, worked as a catalyst. Simons had ventured to use Mozart in his very early pieces. In *Solitude / Im Auge Gottes* this composer appears once again, though now alongside the industrial rock group *Einstürzende Neubauten*. From then on Mozart made regular appearances and Simons exploited his emotional intensity and compositional inventiveness to the full; *Grace*, for example, was inspired by Mozart's *Great Mass in C*. All his attention was focussed on the beauty of the dance, surprisingly lyrical adagios with a powerful emotional effect. This made it clear how far Simons had moved away from his teacher. He did the same again in *Song*, whose basis was formed by extracts from *Così fan tutte* and verses from the twelfth-century Persian Omar Khayyam on leave-taking and the transience of life. Since then Simons has referred to dance as 'sculpting time, space and energy' with our bodies and our souls'. One recognises this addition in the mature dance idiom: it is made vivid by the academic lines of stretched legs and extreme balance. At the same time there are also twisted poses - the torso is turned along the axis of the body, a hip is raised, a foot curved inward. He alternated complex work for the group, with rapid phrases for the legs and fitful arm movements, with slowed-down adagios for a soloist or a couple. These contrasts have a dramatic effect: aggression is contrasted with tenderness, anxiety with resignation.

The stage designs have also gradually changed. In the nineties, the neoconstructivist designs by Andrew Lord and Mark Lancester and the colourful ones by

Photo S. Vanfleteren

Charles Atlas and Roe Aldarada gave way to the streamlined skintight outfits that Simons devised with the dressmaker Edith Ordelman. Light increasingly replaced sets. A refined *chiaroscuro* brought out the spatiality of the choreography. Like black and white, other elements created contrasts too: deafening music alternated with silences, the intensity of a duet with the hectic group passages. Light, sound, image and dance logically interlocked like the fish and birds in M.C. Escher's mathematical graphic art.

Despite this, experimentation continued to be the thread running through Simons' work in the nineties: he based *GOD / DOG Variations* on lighting contrasts and the 'reversal of dance' (what the feet usually do, for example, was now intended for the hands, and *vice versa*). In *Composition for Dancers and Color* the dancers controlled and disrupted the lighting and sound by means of sensors. Each performance of *Through the Wall* started with a different part, so that the choreography 'shifted'. The second part of *Northern Light* was danced on a circular area divided in two by a line lying north-south, so that in each theatre the spatial focus changed. And in *The Idea of Order*, order plays a principal role; it is able to divide, double, reassemble and weave light, colour, sound and dance into a coherent carpet.

**IN THE ROOM
THE WOMEN COME
AND GO TALKING OF
MICHELANGELO, 2001**
Photo R. Benschop

Simons once listed his great examples: Cunningham, Balanchine and the dancer Nijinsky. The first two are obvious. The last represents the inspiring performance. His co-creators are also of considerable importance: Tim Persent, Ty Boomershine and Raymond Esterhuizen. Yet Simons' true muses are women dancers: the level-headed Ellen van Schuylenburch, the virtuoso Brenda Daniëls, the dramatic Joke Zijlstra, the sensual Gaby Allard and the serene Caroline Harder.

TON SIMONS
Beesel, b. 1948

EDUCATION AND CAREER
Studied at the *Rotterdamse Dansacademie* and among other places at the *Merce Cunningham Studio* in New York.

Worked as a dancer and choreographer at *Werkcentrum Dans* and then returned to New York.
In 1986 founded *Ton Simons and Dancers* in New York (dissolved in 1996).
Created choreographic pieces at *Werkcentrum Dans / De Rotterdamse Dansgroep* (DRD).
In 1987 became resident choreographer at *De Rotterdamse Dansgroep* and was appointed artistic director in 1999 (*De Rotterdamse Dansgroep* is now called *Dance Works Rotterdam*).

WORKS
31 Simple Steps, 1975; *Jumble*, 1978; *Commonplace quintet*, 1980; *Rondo*, 1984; *The Palace at 4 A.M. / Spinoza Variations* 1987; *Materia prima*, 1988; *Solitude / Im Auge Gottes*, 1989; *Grace*, 1989; *The Idea of Order*, 1993; *GOD / DOG Variations*, 1994; *Composition for Dancers and Color*, 1995; *Song*, 1996; *Through the Wall*, 1997; *Northern Light*, 2000; *In the Room the Women Come and Go Talking of Michelangelo,* 2001; *Gate to Heaven Road*, 2002; *Eye in All*, 2002; *Scoreline set*, 2002

BIBLIOGRAPHY
Pierre Lartigue, *Le bel aujourd'hui*, in *Festival d'Automne à Paris 1972-1982*, Paris, 1983.
Jan Baart, *International Dictionary of Modern Dance*, under 'Simons', Detroit, 1998.
K. Gosschalk and E. Quint*, Moed en avontuur. Käthy Gosschalk: 25 jaar Werkcentrum Dans / De Rotterdamse Dansgroep*, Amsterdam, 1999.
Marilyn Hunt, 'Ton Simons – Soho to Seattle', in *Dance Magazine*, May 1999.

FILMS - VIDEOS - TELEVISION RECORDINGS
The Palace at 4 A.M. / Spinoza Variations, VPRO; *In the Studio, Part I*, NPS, 1993; *Still Life III*, NPS, 2001

ADDRESS
Dance Works Rotterdam, 's-Gravendijkwal 58 A, NL-3014 EE Rotterdam
Tel.: +31 (0)10 4 364 511
Fax: +31 (0)10 4 364 147
info@danceworksrotterdam.nl
www.danceworksrotterdam.nl

Piet Rogie

For Piet Rogie, art and dance go hand in hand. He trained in both disciplines and still practises both. In the end, dance won out as a profession, though Rogie always tries to connect the two in one way or another. His set and lighting designs, which give his modern dance a character entirely its own, act as a link.

At the start of his career, the relationship between art and dance was still quite concrete. In *De bron der inspiratie* (The Source of Inspiration) he gave the Artist and the Muse an allegorical role; in addition we heard quotations from the painters Rob Scholte and Marlene Dumas about their sources of inspiration. His attempt to interweave dance and art went wrong, however, because the necessary dynamic was lacking. He shifted the emphasis to dance but continued to refer to painterly concepts. One of the motifs in *Clemens' kamer* (Clemens' Room) was the pietà, followed later by models and still-lifes.

Literature was from the very beginning his second starting point. Poetry and passages and characters from world literature provided a loose thread running through his 'narrative' dance pieces. With the playwright Rob de Graaf, for example, he created a trilogy based on the myth of Bluebeard, taking Bartók's opera as the musical foundation. Part One, an introspective solo called *Archief* that Rogie danced himself, was about the danger of seeking and the loneliness of the main character. In *Bulletin*, seven women artists from Rotterdam, colleagues of Rogie's, commented on the topic of men (and their violence) versus women. The third part, *Judit*, the most dramatic and most suitable for dance, focussed on Bluebeard's unhappy beloved. Whispering about dreams and desires was interspersed with a sound collage including excerpts from Bartók.

In the early 1990s he modified this predominantly theatrical line to a dance-oriented approach, with music his main source of inspiration. When it came to music, Rogie's tastes were refined and eclectic. He alternated Bach with *Abba* and Beck (*Nondescript*). Music became a structuring element. In his group piece *Klavier LIVE*, set to piano music by Bach, Beethoven, Schoenberg, Satie, Cage and Szymanovsky, he emerged as a true creator of musical ballets. Nevertheless, his choreographic works were never simply a visualisation of the music. There are always themes, more or less pronounced, that colour the atmosphere.

One latent theme always to be found is eroticism, which Rogie experiences as a complex set of feelings of love. He made reference to this as early as *Kleine oefeningen* (Little Exercises, 1985). Later, passion and a certain fear of women grew into *leitmotifs*. In *Naakt* (Nude) he draped the dancers Kirstin de Groot and Gaby Sund over bare beds; in *Nondescript* he played off a hot-tempered Laura Moro against a cool Johanna Laber, while he himself watched out of the corner of his eye. With Eros comes Thanatos, in Rogie's work too. The set for *Nondescript* comprised transparent panels with negative photographic images of human skeletons printed on them. The naked Rogie occasionally stood just in front of them and life and death then appeared to coincide. His symbols of death are not frightening, however. They seem more like a skull in a *vanitas* still-life, as beautiful as they are symbolic.

Rogie's dance deals implicitly with the relationship between the artist and his muse and / or choreographer and dancer. He has developed this concept in several duets. In *Cargo / Montage*, this relationship (between Rogie and Laber) was prima-

Photo S. Vanfleteren

rily one of companionship, while in *Naast* (Next), also Rogie and Laber, it was rather aloof.

In recent years he has focussed on the body's expression, without using the usual means of making feelings explicit. Taking a verse by Paul van Ostaijen as his thread ('I want to be naked / and make a start'), he shows this body naked and unadorned. In *Lichaam* (Body) he brings the smooth bodies of young dancers face to face with the wrinkled bodies of elderly nude models. In *Model* he has professional nude models adopt classical poses, lying and sitting, and choreographs frisky young women dancers around them. He shows their vulnerability, beauty and mortality in the folds of the skin. The fate of the body in *Tragic Torso*, inspired by Francis Bacon's paintings, is more dramatic. In this group piece, as the realm of eroticism and death, decay and deformation, lit in macabre red and blue, Rogie shows violent emotions, aggression, rage and fear, kept in check by a fragile frame as its scenery.

Rogie is not a choreographer who is concerned solely with steps. He has nevertheless developed an identifiable idiom, in the first place for himself. In his solo piece *Cargo*, this was a faltering, almost nonchalant dance idiom in which his doubts, melancholy and irony deliberately showed through. For other dancers he

TRAGIC TORSO, 2001

Photo S. van Schouwen

created more confident steps in a modern idiom with a clear classical line and beauty, with small rapid steps set against long poses and arabesques. Classical technique provides him with the neutral expression and purity he is looking for. Starting with this, he adds colour to the dance, but in not too pronounced a way. He prefers to allow sensuality or vulnerability to express itself naturally on the basis of a gentle line, which brings him close to the mildly spiritually-tinged expressionism that is appearing as a new trend among young choreographers. He has recently collaborated with two such, Bruno Listopad and Megumi Nakamura.

PIET ROGIE
Avelgem (Belgium), b. 1954

EDUCATION AND CAREER
Studied at the *Academie voor Schone Kunsten* in Gent and at the *Koninklijke Balletschool* in Antwerp.

In 1979 established himself in Rotterdam as a dancer, choreographer, set & lighting designer. Made his choreographic debut in 1981 (*Celcius Blanco*).
From 1986 to 1989 was artistic director of the *Penta Theater*, from 1989 to 1997 of *Compagnie Peter Bulcaen* (for one year jointly with Hans Tuerlings) and since 1997 of *Rogie & Company*.

WORKS
Celcius Blanco, 1981; *Kleine oefeningen*, 1985; *De bron der inspiratie*, 1986; *Bleekgoud*, 1988; *Clemens' kamer*, 1989; *Homo Fragilis of de benen van een vrouw / Cargo*, 1989; *Kataloog* (in association with Hans Tuerlings), 1990; *Mutterseelenallein*, 1990; *Multipel*, 1991; *Kaiet – Kaiet* (in association with Arne Sierens), 1992; *Archief, Opéra laconique de l'école Faux-Naif*, 1993; *Naakt*, 1993; *Bulletin*, 1993; *Judit*, 1994; *Cargo / Montage,* 1995; *Naast*, 1996; *Nondescript,* 1997; *Klavier LIVE*, 1997; *Lichaam*, 1998; *Model*, 1999; *State of the Art: Panorama*, 1999 and *Icoon*, 2000; *Tragic Torso*, 2001; *Space of the Shadows*, 2002; *To Act, I Come*, 2002; *WO / MAN*, 2002

BIBLIOGRAPHY
Floris Brester, 'Ik wil mensen zien, geen dansers – Piet Rogie bekroond voor zijn hele choreografische oeuvre', in *NRC Handelsblad*, 31 October 1997.
Ariejan Korteweg, 'De danser wordt een zwerver', in *de Volkskrant*, 6 February 1998.
Gabriël Smeets, 'Mijn knieën redden het niet meer', in *TM*, October 2001.

FILMS - VIDEOS - TELEVISION recordings
Cargo, NPS / Basement, 1989; *Het geheim van de denkende danser*, NPS / Basement, 1998; Tragic Torso, NPS, 2002

ADDRESS
Rogie & Company, Voorhaven 21, NL-3025 HC Rotterdam
Tel.: +31 (0)10 244 09 68
Fax: +31 (0)10 244 09 69
info@rogie-company.nl
www.rogie-company.nl

Ed Wubbe

Ed Wubbe once named *Rameau* and *Kathleen* as his essential ballets, because of their extreme, dramatic nature. They thereby mark the musical and theatrical lines along which his work unfolds. *Rameau* represents the dancing-to-music line, which he initiated in ballets set to Händel (*Messiah*) and Vivaldi (*Nisi Dominus*), both of which were sparkling choreographic works that accentuated the energy and dynamics of the music, and continued in *Parts* and *Perfect Skin*, set to Bach. However, something of the drama of *Kathleen*, which turned out to be the overture to a theatrical line, also lay dormant in *Rameau*. He combined his fascination for the cool, formal harpsichord music of the baroque composer Rameau with the last days of courtly music and thereby to the disenchantment of the French nobility waiting resignedly for the guillotine. This explains why some of the dancers, slightly bored, watch the wilful duets and solos performed by dancers in leather jackets and sturdy boots.

In *Rameau*, Wubbe made a deep scratch in the gloss of the ballet aesthetics he had been given in his classical training and as a dancer and choreographer at the *Nederlands Dans Theater* and *Introdans*. Initially, he was still very much influenced by Kylián. *White Streams*, set to Arvo Pärt, was a successful example of a music ballet in which the continuous flow of movements in an organic dance idiom yielded a fine lyrical image. By contrast, his idiom became angular and sharp when he worked with the classical dancers of the *Scapino Ballet* and learned to make use of their dancing in ballet slippers, as in *Nisi Dominus*, *Rameau*, *Parts* and *Perfect Skin*.

Kathleen was a real turning-point, as an intense dance ritual set to pop music by Godflesh, with vivacious trios, aggressive group dances and a gripping male solo. This was a powerful work that displayed a pessimistic nihilism on which it made implicit comment. This contemporary *West Side Story* was also a statement by a choreographer who had been able to free himself entirely from the tradition that had characterised the *Scapino* youth ballet company since its founding in 1945. No subsequent ballet was as furious as *Kathleen*. Even his *Le Sacre du printemps* was a refined combination of dance, music, light and set, for which he deliberately chose not Stravinsky's violent orchestral work but Maarten Bon's subtle adaptation for pianos.

His theatrical work was cerebral rather than compelling, and was impressionist in tone as a result of its light dance idiom and associative storyline. For example, he set *Romeo & Julia* to an amalgam of non-western music - love songs - and concentrated the story into twelve scenes. Writings by Shakespeare, Yourcenar, Da Vinci and Marinetti touched upon the original love tragedy. The love duet - the balcony scene - was a particular scorcher, after which the vengeful Tybalt made sure the burning love charred into a pile of smouldering ash. *The Schliemann Pieces* focussed on the passion with which the amateur archaeologist Schliemann once sought Troy. Excerpts from his diary and from the *Iliad* were quoted. Apart from Schliemann, the Greek beauty Sophia was also identifiable as a character.

The leading character's feverish quest seemed to represent the equally single-minded way Wubbe sought a formula for making theatrical work that was not predictable. He was more successful at this in *Nico*, about the life and music of the legendary singer. Its great asset was the music specially composed by John Cale,

Photo S. Vanfleteren

a member of The Velvet Underground at the time and a former lover of Nico's. Cale's music was alternated with songs by Nico on tape. One could follow the course of Nico's life in the danced scenes, without resort to anecdote: the Chelsea Girl in New York who created a furore with her organ and seasoned singing in the seventies, until her sojourn and death on Ibiza. This piece, where music, dance and drama were all of a piece, was made especially gripping by the performance of Beth Bartholomew.

Rosary was a successful example of the new style of music ballet. It was a sparkling group work that playfully and organically translated the emotions from Schubert's *String Quartet in C*. With thanks to the dancers, who creamed off the articulated movements of the legs and fitful turns of the torso and in their stock-inged feet made them appear feather-light. An utterly lyrical ballet that nevertheless did not come across as overly fragrant and in which he proved his mature ability as a creator of pure dance constructions and duets.

As a modern choreographer and leader of the leading *Scapino* company, now brought up to date, Wubbe wants to establish links with other disciplines and art institutions in Rotterdam. He has for example collaborated with Winy Maas of the MVRDV firm of architects. Using computer graphics, designers translated her

MANYFACTS, 2001
Photo H. Gerritsen

stratified concept of 'the stacked city' into a virtual stage set, a kaleidoscopic panorama of abstract images in which dancers performed like symbols of the human
dimension. *Manyfacts, Life in the 3D City* was about the interaction between anonymous and personal, abstraction and emotion. Wubbe wants to express this personal aspect in his dances. His classically-based modern dance is nevertheless highly
stylised, but this does not stop the dancers from making their own mark on it: in the
past there were Charlotte Baines and Keith-Derrick Randolph, and now, together
with Mischa van Leeuwen and Bonnie Doets there are another twenty-two high-
quality expressive dancers.

ED WUBBE

Nieuwer Amstel, b. 1957

EDUCATION AND CAREER

Studied at the *Scapino Dansacademie* in Amsterdam.

Worked first as a dancer with *Springplank* (junior group of the *Nederlands Dans Theater*) and at the *Werkcentrum Dans*.
Made his choreographic debut in 1981 (*Subterranians*).
Was resident choreographer at *Introdans* and *Scapino Ballet (Rotterdam)*.
Since 1993 has been artistic director of *Scapino Ballet (Rotterdam)*.

WORKS

Subterranians, 1981; *Afstand*, 1982; *White Streams,* 1986; *Messiah,* 1988; *De dood en het meisje,* 1989; *Nisi Dominus*, 1989; *Rameau*, 1990; *Parts*, 1991; *Perfect Skin,* 1991, 1992, full-length programme 1993; *Kathleen*, 1992, full-length programme 1994; *Romeo & Julia*, 1995; *Le Sacre du printemps*, 1996; *Nico*, 1997; *The Schliemann Pieces*, 1998; *Single Manoeuvres,* 1999; *Rosary*, 2000; *Plot*, 2000; *Manyfacts*, 2001; *Out of China*, 2002; *Tsjaikovski p.i.*, 2002

BIBLIOGRAPHY

Joyce Roodnat, 'Die passen houdt Keith wel in zijn benen', in *NRC Handelsblad*, 26 February 1993.
Eva van Schaik, 'Ik maak Scapino tot de Wubbe Dance Company', in *Trouw*, 8 April 1993.
Ariejan Korteweg, 'Aan Scapino is alles nieuw, behalve de naam', in *de Volkskrant*, 19 August 1994.

FILMS - VIDEOS - TELEVISION RECORDINGS

White Streams, NOS, 1991; *Cult*, VARA, 1991; *The Sorceress* (with Kiri Te Kanawa and *Het Natio-nale Ballet*), NOS, 1992; *Kathleen*, NPS, 1993; *Single Manoeuvres*, NPS, 2000; *Enclosed*, NPS / BBC, 2000; *LOST*, NPS, 2001

ADDRESS

Scapino Ballet Rotterdam, Eendrachtsstraat 8, NL-3012 XL Rotterdam
Tel.: +31 (0)10 414 24 14
Fax: +31 (0)10 413 22 50
info@scapinoballet.nl
www.scapinoballet.nl

Itzik Galili

Itzik Galili started dancing relatively late in life, which is quite unusual. His background is equally unusual, and he likes to shroud it in mystery. One story is that he grew up in the backstreets of Tel Aviv, was uncontrollable, had to be sent into care, had lived on the street since he was twelve and after his army service went from one dead-end job to another. Another story has it that after three years of army service he wanted to travel and study psychology and to finance this worked as a qualified poodle trimmer. From then on the stories run parallel: he started doing folk dancing and at the age of twenty-two his dancing talent was discovered and he was promptly given a place in the junior section of the *Batsheva Dance Company*. Two years later he was dancing with the main group and won a prize with his choreographic debut.

His progress as a choreographer in the Netherlands was miraculously rapid. He and his work are characterised both by mystery - there are also two versions of his move to the Netherlands (either for love or away from the Gulf War) - and by a realistic will-power. His work is not always equally unambiguous and also fluctuates in its theatrical intensity.

His initial work was light; for instance, *The Butterfly Effect*, an inventive little construction with a changeable form, for three dancers and three bricks. It was not plagiarism (see Vandekeybus) as was briefly supposed, but it was clearly influenced by the work of the Israeli choreographer Daniel Ezralow, his colleague in that country. By contrast, the realism of *Ma's Bandage*, about rape and abuse, makes it a difficult piece. Galili is often able to strike a balance between emotionality and perspective, and intuition and intellect.

His lively imagination, expressive dreams and real experiences provide him with his ideas. For example, his debut, *Double Time* - a sham fight between two men, was about seeing his brother again after having lost touch with him for years. His recollections of a woman street-vendor led to a witty tribute to the Yiddishe mamma in *Through Nana's Eyes*. He portrayed his then relationship with the dancer Jennifer Hanna in *When You See God, Tell Him*. In simple movements this duet evokes love and happiness, doubt and conflict, and reconciliation and acceptance, all without sentiment or cliché. The music supplies a second layer. A text is woven into Scott Johnson's melancholic *Soliloquy*, a speech made by the American journalist I.F. Stone in 1983, which contains a plea for reason and reconciliation. Warning words about the dangerous struggle between Israelis and Palestinians coincide with gestures suggesting shooting. It is well done in the sense that the parallel between their personal struggle and the international conflicts does not appear forced. It is an expressive dance duet and at the same time a humanist statement. The duet *Between L...*, for Anne Affourtit and Derrick Brown, was a lighter variation on this theme. They comment on their relationship in the form of a dialogue while simultaneously illustrating it: on sex, the grind of everyday life and dance routines it is fairly innocent, but when the bloody conflict between the Hutus and the Tutsis is mentioned in passing, all movement is briefly paralysed.

Galili does not feel tied to any traditions and is open to experiment. This is apparent in *Chronocration*, which he made with the avant-garde composer Gene Carl. Although the original idea of the audience being able to influence the music

Photo S. Vanfleteren

and dance in the course of the performance was abandoned, this piece was quite exceptional because the fourteen dancers, on a sprung mattress, played the seven grand pianos and a violin themselves. When they collaborated a second time, on *Below Paradise*, the music and the dance went too much their own way. His coproduction with *Ginko*, four elderly Japanese dancers, also partly created the fragile atmosphere he seeks, as well as the charm of childhood memories.

Galili's restless quest can sometimes lead to such absurd work as *The Familiar Stranger*. *For Heaven's Sake*, by contrast, was crystal clear, and was prompted by rage and fear, feelings that were activated so much more after September 11. The piece opens roughly, with the dancers turning over and over; it represents flogging and torture and is full of associations of violence. The scene in which dancers stumble along on prostheses, like hunted, wounded game, is heart-rending. Melancholy oriental sounds tell us how peaceful it could be, but a monologue about the massacre in Chatila, spat out by Stephen Shropshire, shows how far off this peace still is; since September 11 it is further away than ever.

Even in his theatrical work, the power of the images is as important as the expressiveness of the dance itself. It is vital and worldly: impulsive in the torso and with both feet planted firmly on the ground. In this respect his work seems akin to

FOR HEAVEN'S SAKE,

2001

Photo K. Zwaneveld

the style of Ohad Naharin, which was once characterised as 'the style of the survivors'. Galili's Mediterranean temperament, his drive and passion, poetry and humour are also reflected in his work, which has been successful in several European countries.

In the meantime the Groningen polders now house a real Israeli colony, because a relatively large number of his dancers are Israeli. Roni Haver and Guy Vaizman have now also made a successful debut as a choreographic duo, whereby Galili's intention of stimulating dance has been achieved.

ITZIK GALILI
Tel Aviv (Israel), b. 1961

CAREER
Dancer with the Israeli companies *Bat Dor Dance Company* and *Batsheva Dance Company*.
Made his choreographic debut in 1990 (*Double Time*).
In 1990 settled in the Netherlands and in 1992 founded *Galili Dance*.
Since 1998 has been artistic director of *Galili Dance* / *Noord-Nederlandse Dansgroep*.

WORKS
Double Time, 1990; *Old Cartoon*, 1990; *The Butterfly Effect*, 1990; *Trekidos*, 1991; *Blind Kingdom*, 1992; *When You See God, Tell Him*, 1993; *Perureim*, 1993; *Ma's Bandage*, 1994; *Uhlai*, 1995; *Between L...*, 1995; *Through Nana's Eyes*, 1995; *Chronocration*, 1996; *Below Paradise*, 1997; *See under X*, 1997; *The Familiar Stranger*, 1998; *The Drunken Garden*, 1999; *Things I Told Nobody* (in association with *Ginko*), 2000; *For Heaven's Sake* (in association with *Gulbenkian Ballet*), 2001; *There, There Is*, 2002

BIBLIOGRAPHY
Margriet Oostveen, 'Hij weet zich van geluk geen raad', in *NRC Handelsblad*, 13 September 1996.
Annette Embrechts, 'Wees aardig, wees alleen', in *de Volkskrant*, 11 September 1998.
Lucia van Heteren, 'De dag nadat de wereld stilstond', in *TM*, December 2001 / January 2002.

FILMS - VIDEOS - TELEVISION RECORDINGS
When You See God, Tell Him, NPS, 1994; *Between L...*, NPS, 1995; *Chronocration*, NPS, 1996; *Come Across*, NPS / BBC, 2000; *For Heaven's Sake*, NPS, 2002

ADDRESS
Galili Dance / Noord-Nederlandse Dansgroep, Postbus 1517, NL-9701 BM Groningen
Tel.: +31 (0)50 579 94 41
Fax: +31 (0)50 579 94 62
info@nnd.nl
www.galilidance.com

Andrea Leine & Harijono Roebana

Harijono Roebana was a student of philosophy, interested in life's great questions, and Andrea Leine was a ballet pupil. Nothing indicated that they would create a furore as a duo of contemporary choreographers, even beyond the boundaries of the Netherlands. Roebana started his training in modern dance late in the day. Once he had started in that direction, he soon took up choreography. His dance is striking for its violent angular movements, contrariness and irony. Leine joined him for *Waldo*, as a dancer and assistant. Two productions later she was his co-choreographer. Roebana's theatrical irony is gradually giving way to pure dance. Andrea Leine contributes a rounded and organic style of movement that results from her physique. Their idiom has become significantly more polished, although Roebana's impulsive swipes remain part of it. Both continue to dance in the pieces they have choreographed.

Leine & Roebana work on the basis of intellect and intuition, both conceptually and emotionally. Like others of their generation, they want to get away from the formal idiom of the postmodernists without returning to an explicit expressionism, and are looking for a way to reconcile strict form with dance that radiates emotion.

Their work initially showed traces of theatricality, as in *Suites (Dansen voor de koningin)* (Dances for the Queen) and *The Circle Effect*. The accent has gradually shifted to pure dance and an homogeneous style has emerged. This became clear for the first time in *If We Could Only If We Could*, a modest group work that contained many of the components of their idiom. Upper bodies and arms bent and turned in circles and ovals and legs made rotating movements from the hip joint (this joint is accentuated in their work). This roundness brings a breath of air into their dance. Yet there are still sharp and disrupting movements: limbs that crack, feet and arms that shoot out fitfully, like points in a mainly smooth whole. The latter arises because they sometimes set off a chain reaction from a particular point in the body. They often steer the dance from the torso and stay close to the ground. This earthiness and roundness makes the dance sensual. A game of deceleration and acceleration, of vigorous and abrupt starts or, by contrast, gentle skimming, lends dynamism to their dance. Because they do not build in any strict spatial compositions - they usually dance in loose formations, with short alternating solos, duets, trios and passages in unison - their choreography is reminiscent of Kandinsky's playful abstract geometry.

Their idiom - so it is said - seeks a path through the tension between order and chaos, rules and freedom, choreographic structure and the dancers' inner motivation. Apart from the choreographers, in recent years these dancers have included Ty Boomershine, Janine Dijkmeijer, Mischa van Dullemen, Andreas Fratzl, Tim Persent and Ederson Rodrigues Xavier. Although Leine & Roebana come up with a new well-defined idea for each production, improvisation forms an essential part of their choreography. The dance bears traces of the intentions of the dancers themselves. This personal element has been a pronounced presence since *Tales of Eversion*. The dancers colour in their movements on the spot, fluently or abruptly, depending on their mood.

Leine & Roebana's method has been influenced by Cunningham (chance, autonomy) and Forsythe (improvisation in accordance with his analytical decon-

structional model). In addition, the duo uses 'images' that elicit movement: the course of a ball circling a body yields an undulating movement, for example. It is a method the American postmodernist Trisha Brown uses. They also invent numerous approaches of their own: if a dancer in a duet thwarts his partner, this may evoke a distorted image.

Ideas like this are common in contemporary modern dance and produce comparable dance styles. But the work of Leine & Roebana stands out. Their experimental quest for the ideal dance idiom is accompanied by an exploration of the relationship between dance and music. Their rather unusual choice of music was already apparent in *Tales of Eversion*, which included John Zorn, Gavin Bryars and Edgar Varèse's modern classic *Ionisation*. This element was enhanced by a course on composition and choreography at Wakefield in the United Kingdom. In *Byrd* they introduced the sound of the virginal into contemporary compositions by Iannis Kyriakides. In *S/he* they explored the viola da gamba because of its soft, intimate timbre. They are not however aiming for a visualisation of the music, but enter into dialogue with it, literally in fact, since they share the stage with the musicians. Early music appeals to them especially, because of its reconciliation of strict form with emotionality. They want the emotions to come through in their dance in a similar way.

Conversely, their work has not gone unnoticed in musical circles. Josep Vincent, the leader of the *Slagwerkgroep Amsterdam* (Amsterdam Percussion Group), initiated their collaboration on *Eye in All*, in which *Dance Works* also participated. Leine & Roebana go for compelling percussion compositions by Steve Reich, Iannis Xenakis and Pierre Boulez. Their performances are certainly exciting, though details may be lost on larger stages. Leine & Roebana's dance seems to benefit from the intimacy of smaller auditoriums. The nuances that dancers put into their performances on the spot make an essential contribution to the generous expression of this charming twenty-first century chamber dance.

ANDREA LEINE
Amsterdam, b. 1966

Studied at the *Scapino dansacademie* in Amsterdam (classical ballet performance) and at the *Rotterdamse Dansacademie* (classical ballet and modern dance performance).

Since 1992 has been a dancer and co-choreographer with *Leine & Roebana*.

HARIJONO ROEBANA
Amsterdam, b. 1955

Graduated from the *Opleiding Moderne Dans* in Amsterdam.
Also studied philosophy, theatre studies and musicology.

Founded the *Date* company in 1983.
Made his choreographic debut in 1988 (*Mei*).
Since 1992 has been a dancer and co-choreographer with *Leine & Roebana*.

WORKS
Suites (Dansen voor de koningin), 1993; *The Circle Effect*, 1995; *If We Could Only If We Could*, 1995; *Tales of Eversion*, 1997; *No*, 1998; *Byrd*, 1999; *Cantus Firmus*, 2000; *S/he*, 2001; *Eye in All*, 2002; *Point Of View of nobody in particular*, 2002

BIBLIOGRAPHY
Myriam van Imschoot, 'A Ship that Sails out and Finds Itself in a Storm', in *Carnet*, 1996.
Mirjam van der Linden, 'Mastering a Powerful Vocabulary', in *Carnet*, 1998.
Jacqueline Algra, 'Wij maken muziek en dans op menselijk formaat', in *TM*, 2001, no. 2.

FILMS - VIDEOS - TELEVISION RECORDINGS
E pur si muove, Bergen, 1993; *If We Could Only If We Could*, NPS, 1996; *Sulphur*, NPS, 2000

ADDRESS
Stichting Date, Wg-Plein 363, NL-1054 SG Amsterdam
Tel.: +31 (0)20 489 38 20
Fax: +31 (0)20 489 38 21
dans@leineroebana.com

Conny Janssen

Conny Janssen bases her work on human motivations: feeling and intuition, human forms of contact, aggression and vulnerability are the sources of her dance. In the beginning it was slightly anecdotal. She put her outrage over abuses into *Welk een eer voor het vaderland te mogen sterven* (What an Honour to be Able to Die for One's Country). *A Silent Place to Rest* arose out of the lament that we live in a hectic world and long for intimacy and security. *Instinct* was a highly emotionally-charged piece in which she portrayed the dark sides of relationships whose main motives are passion, aggression and distrust, and the loner as the victim of the group. This was her reaction to anonymous street violence. Her most realistic ballet so far has been *Vijzel*, the background to which was personal. In fact her father, a former factory manager, even appeared on the posters. In a theatrical setting - a factory canteen in the fifties - she sketched the lives and loves of burly workers and factory girls. This theatricality made *Vijzel* (tr. Mortar) quite exceptional but contained a theme that developed into a lasting motif.

Her work is often tinged with nostalgia, involving vague recollections and the feelings that go with them. She has developed these reminiscences with a whole range of nuances. *Oktober*, for example, is about an autumnal sort of longing. For this group piece she chose dark music by Henryk Gorécki and Lou Reed and added melancholy harmonica playing by one of the dancers. The eye-catcher was the stage setting, a dark facade on a square where people encountered one another. This later changed into a colourful facade comprising doors behind which the people disappeared one by one. The duets were about a certain hankering for each other, and about reaching out for one another. The most evocative scene was that in which sultry late-summer chirping filled the half-darkened stage, coming from Chinese cricket-cages that the dancers wore on their backs.

Álbum Familiar evoked a slightly lighter, nostalgic atmosphere using music from times past: mediaeval music, creaky tangos by Carlos Gardel and songs by Leonard Cohen. The set, a gallery of portrait photos above a row of chairs, subtly suggested a dancing club, one of those you can visit till the early hours. Watching and being watched while dancing, that's what this charming gem for seven dancers was all about. The choreography showed all the velvet-soft forms of duet and complex trios from her inventive dance vocabulary.

Álbum Familiar was made very quickly and illustrates her method. She usually has a vague idea and develops it in the studio in collaboration with the dancers, by focussed improvisation and other means. The outline is slowly filled in to form a clear image. Some of this associative improvisation remains in the dance, because it always comes across as playful, even though the choreography has been fixed. The best aspect of Janssen's work is her dance idiom, which is full of contrasts and yet homogeneous. She organically links long, supple movements to fitful twists of the arms and legs. Powerfully sharp and impulsive movements are made loosely and fluently. And despite its earthy nature her dance is light-footed. She also handles serious themes with lightness. In complex partner passages for two or three she moulds the bodies into sculptural formations that seem more like pitch-stone than granite. She alternates this complexity with unisonous passages that offer a clear view. The dance still remains at the fore even in a theatrical context.

Photo S. Vanfleteren

The robustness and sensuality of her idiom comes partly from the dancers. In addition to their technique, she also selects them for their presence and temperament. She considers the chemistry between the dancers, and between them and her, to be of crucial importance. Several of them - Jens van Daele, Froilan Medina Hernandez and Iris Reyes - have helped shape her style.

She recently worked with the hiphop group *010 BBoyz*. *Meet me, a Dancer* was about the confrontation between her polished modern idiom and the raw acrobatics of the street. 'Encounters' were also the main element in *Number One*, as well as the loner versus the group. The duets expressed fine nuances of feeling: from sweet, gentle lyricism to gritty contrariness. In the beginning the dream-like set was dominant, but half-pipes gradually gave the dancers the opportunity to climb, slide, roll and skate on their stockinged feet to their heart's content.

Janssen has a broad and varied taste in music. Her choices range from Renaissance and classical (Händel, Bach) to modern (Glass) and pop. She has also collaborated with *Yens & Yens* and *Paleis van Boem*. Very occasionally the music has been the main source of inspiration, as in *Made to Measure*, set to Bach's *St John Passion* and Lambarena's Afro version of it, and in *De zuchten van Rameau* (The Sighs of Rameau) the basis was a composition by Jacob ter Veldhuis. More

NUMBER ONE, 2002
Photo C. van Hees

often, however, the role of the music is to enhance the atmosphere, although its rhythm always provides the momentum. Janssens' work is made accessible by the dynamic of her style and because it is emotionally identifiable. Her involvement and social engagement are reflected in it, as are her matter-of-factness and realism. *Conny Janssen Danst*, the company she set up in 1992, supplies a full and effervescent jazzy note in a predominantly conceptual modern dance scene.

CONNY JANSSEN
Rotterdam, b. 1958

EDUCATION AND CAREER
Studied at the *Rotterdamse Dansacademie*.

From 1982 to 1990 was a dancer with *Djazzex*.
Made her choreographic debut there in 1988 (*The Undertow*).
In 1992 founded *Conny Janssen Danst* (in association with *Impresariaat Wim Visser*).

WORKS
Eloï, eloï 1991; *Moving Target*, 1993; *The Unanswered Question*, 1994; *Frames per Second*, 1995; *In het voorbijgaan*, 1995; *A Silent Place to Rest*, 1995; *Welk een eer voor het vaderland te mogen sterven*, 1996; *Made to Measure*, 1998; *Vijzel*, 1999; *Kus van een vis*, 1999; *Oktober*, 1999; *Instinct*, 2000; *De zuchten van Rameau*, 2000; *Meander*, 2001; *Álbum Familiar*, 2001; *Meet Me, a Dancer*, 2001; *Number One*, 2002; *Vuil & Glass*, 2002

BIBLIOGRAPHY
Hans den Hartog Jager, 'Het duet van verlangen', in *NRC Handelsblad*, 19 February 1999.
Isabella Lanz, 'Driedelig dansproject in Rotterdam', in *NRC Handelsblad*, 4 February 2001.
Irene Start, 'Voortdurend afscheid nemen', in *Dans,* February 2002.

FILMS - VIDEOS - TELEVISION RECORDINGS
A Silent Place to Rest, NPS, 1998; *Oktober*, NPS, 1999; *P.*, 2000; *Álbum Familiar*, NPS, 2001

ADDRESS
Conny Janssen Danst, 's-Gravendijkwal 58 B, NL-3002 AH Rotterdam
Tel.: +31 (0)10 452 99 12
Fax: +31 (0)10 241 77 03
info@connyjanssendanst.nl
www.connyjanssendanst.nl

Emio Greco & P.C. Scholten

Wasn't Vaslav Nijinsky the young man who couldn't cope as a dancer amongst a sophisticated public, but in the studio made the dancers so crazy that they danced to Stravinsky's raw chords? Without wanting to proclaim Emio Greco a genius, something in this son of a poor Italian farmer is reminiscent of the legendary star. It's probably the passion. He is acclaimed throughout Europe as a representative of a new conceptual movement that sees the body as a spiritual phenomenon, an image of the spirit become flesh. The German 'Jungians' call this *gestalt*.

Greco only started in ballet when he was twenty-one. The influence of classical dance technique is most visible in the long, open line of his neck and streamlined arm movements. He then picked up ideas on dance and theatre while working with Jan Fabre. Something of Fabre's mythical and sinister images of the world and underworld stuck in his mind, like those the film director David Lynch sketched in *Twin Peaks*. His third teacher, this time for dance idiom, was Teshigawara. Greco adopted to the full his extreme concentration and his balance between apparent weightlessness and an actual connection to the earth.

Greco actively fused these influences into a powerful and individual style, with dance, sound, and set plus lighting as a compact trinity. He is fascinating to watch: he lets his body zigzag like a flash of lightning, stands with his feet on the floor and raises his arms high towards heaven, preferably in acute diagonal positions. He sets his legs wide apart, bends his back in a great curve over them and keeps his arms on his back as if tied. These dramatic poses and evocative gestures are enhanced by his facial expressions, like those of a tormented ascetic who sees fearsome visions. He sometimes hops strangely on the outside of his feet, wobbles and yet reaches to the heavens, sinks into gentle meditative poses or stands motionlessly at the side, like an oriental priest.

Greco creates his work together with the Dutch dramaturge Pieter C. Scholten. Their starting point was a manifesto entitled *Les sept nécessités*. With this declaration of principles they turned against the empty virtuosity of ballet and the formal nature of modern and postmodern dance. Their work can best be described as a spiritually-tinged abstract expressionism. This makes them the indirect heirs to the prewar *Ausdruckstanz* that left its traces in the *butoh* dances of Japan. However, the difference from this expressionism was that it is not Greco's intention to convey feelings or symbolise ideas. He is looking for a direct link between body and mind. In *Fra Cervello e Movimento* he made a theme of this connection between the brain and the body's actions. After the solos *Bianco* and *Rosso*, the duet *Extra Dry* was the crowning glory of the trilogy. In this brotherly duo Greco was joined by the Belgian Andy Deneys, with fine double images and vivid contrasts. These contrasts have characterised all his subsequent work: he parries overwhelming sound by standing stock-still. Curtains of light from high up or low down, from the sides or from upstage, cast dramatic shadows and have a blinding effect. The set itself is by contrast often subtly simple, a rigid framework along the three walls, covered with fabrics that are as shiny, fluffy or creased as the costumes designed by Clifford Portiers. The sweat makes these dress-like robes in coarse-fibred fabrics into a sort of second skin.

Photo S. Vanfleteren

After this successful trilogy, Greco and Scholten created a new series called *Double Points*, the second of which was set to Ravel's surging *Boléro*, spectacular bombastic music that lends itself to being carried along in a stirring whirl of repetition, exactly as Béjart had previously done. But Greco opted to dance in a strip between two bands of light, at the very edge, facing the audience frontally. The 'Italian' *bolero* forms the overture to *Double Points Zero* and its development in *Conjunto di Nero*, his darkest work. The walls were covered in black and as it opened, one of his dancers, Bertha Bermúdez Pascual, danced parts of Fokine's expressionist *Dying Swan* on pointes. Cones of light sliced through the darkness in a design reminiscent of Adolphe Appia's stage settings from around 1920. Again that association with early expressionism. These images were certainly evocative, marked by heavy outlines. His style is called 'extremalism', the dark counterpart to Minimalism. Greco does indeed work on the basis of a limited range of motifs of movement which he then repeats, and sometimes has them performed immediately after or synchronously alongside each other, or simultaneously. His eye for composition is crucial, and this is how he keeps the weighty content well under control.

RIMASTO ORFANO, 2002

Photo J.-P. Stoop /
SOFAM - Belgium

The 'Greco & PC' duo has in the meantime been almost beatified in a philosophical essay that verges on the hysterical, on sacred and profane, transcendent and metaphysical, metaphor, metamorphosis, things Dionysian and Appolinairian. In a series of philosophical clichés, Greco is attributed with almost Messianic qualities. Greco plays with the imposed status in his recent, more restrained group work *Rimasto Orfano*. This is opened by a woman dancer, with a sinister, sensually whispered opening sentence: 'Emio Greco is dead', after which she vanishes and he rises up in her place. Above his head is a flickering light bulb, a symbol of the restless soul of this inspired creator.

EMIO GRECO
Brindisi (Italy), b. 1965

Ballet training in Cannes.

Was a dancer with and assistant to Jan Fabre and danced for Saburo Teshigawara.
In 1995 set up *Emio Greco / PC* (manifesto: *Les sept nécessités*).

PIETER C. SCHOLTEN
Vlaardingen, b. 1962

Studied at the *Academie voor Expressie door Woord en Gebaar* in Kampen.

Was initially dramaturge to the Brazilian choreographer Marcelo Evelin who works in the Netherlands.
In 1995 set up *Emio Greco / PC* (manifesto: *Les sept nécessités*).
Also works as a director.

WORKS
Trilogy: *Fra Cervello e Movimento*: *Bianco*, 1995 - *Rosso*, 1997 - *Extra Dry,* 1999; *Double Points I*, 1998; *Double Points 2*, 1999; *Double Point: Nero*, 2000; *Conjunto de Falda y Chaqueta,* 2000; *Double Points Zero,* 2001; *Conjunto di Nero*, 2001; *Rimasto Orfano,* 2002

BIBLIOGRAPHY
Paul Derksen, 'Fra cervello e movimento', in *Notes*, February 1996.
Michaele Schlagenwerth, 'Das Echo des Körpers – Koffi Kôkô und Emio Greco',
in *Körper.con.text, Das Jahrbuch Ballet / Tanz*, 1999.
Antoon van den Braembussche *It's Life Jim, but Not As We Know It*, Amsterdam, 2001.
Helmut Ploebst, *No Wind, No Word, Neue Choreographie in der Gesellschaft des Spektakels*, Munich, 2001 (in German and English).
Annette Embrechts, 'Goddelijk', in *de Volkskrant*, 6 June 2002.

FILMS - VIDEOS - TELEVISION RECORDINGS
Fra, NPS, 2000; *Double Points I,* NPS, 2001; *Rimasto Orfano*, NPS, 2002

ADDRESS
Emio Greco & PC / Zwaanprodukties
Witte de Withstraat 117 III, NL-1057 XR Amsterdam
Tel.: +31 (0)20 616 72 40
Fax: +31 (0)20 616 72 40
zwaanproductions@compuserve.com
www.emiogrecoandpc.nl

Nanine Linning is among the youngest of the highly-talented choreographers in the Netherlands. She received a great deal of attention very rapidly, particularly after Ed Wubbe appointed her resident choreographer at *Scapino Ballet Rotterdam* in 2001. In her teenage years she took dance expression classes. She learnt traditional dancing at the *Rotterdamse Dansacademie*: classical, modern, composition and improvisation. She did not want to become a dance teacher, but a postgraduate course in choreography was set up more or less at her request, the first such specialised course in the Netherlands. She is a creator more than a dancer. She is interested in pure, abstract dance and in space and structure, which she picked up from her parents, both architects. She took a course at William Forsythe's *Ballett Frankfurt* and assisted in the making of the dance film *From a Classical Position*, a duet by Forsythe, with Dana Caspersen.

Linning incorporated the influence of this style into her debut piece, *Metro*, especially in its fitful, fragmentary physical dance. She is developing an analytical approach, studying the workings of the human body with almost scientific precision; the heart in *Cardiac Motion*, the bone and muscle system in *Anatomism*. She asks herself questions about space, rhythm, volume and layers, just like a constructivist. She also studies the patterns of movement of people in enclosed spaces, like mice in a laboratory. She shares this fascination with structuralist and sociological matters, the beta and alpha in a *pas de deux*, with other young choreographers. Yet her work does not appear dry or sterile, nor does it lack energy and dynamism.

Linning even tailors her solos to the qualities of the dancer for whom they are made. To give two examples, in *Solo* she creates a portrait, set to the music of Arvo Pärt, of the precise dancing of Caroline Harder, and, in *Solo 5.0*, of the expressive passion of Mirjam ter Linden.

Light plays an essential part in her duet *Mono / Stereo*, which she originally danced with Bruno Listopad, and whose revival was danced by the *Scapino* dancers Sandra Marín García and Ederson Rodrigues Xavier. It separates the dancers, but at the start and finish also ties them together. Lying on the ground, they together show their folded hands and arms in the light of a floor spot, which yields an intimate image without the ballast of emotional expression. This introvert duet for a man and a woman was followed by one which in many respects was its counterpart. She made *Karpp...?* for the blonde Mirjan ter Linden and dark Iris Reyes: explosive dance, comradely while yet scoring points off each other, breathtaking in pace, driven along by the music of Jacob ter Veldhuis.

The transition from solos, duets and limited group pieces in a small theatre, to ensemble work on larger stages, must be considerable, but she leapt the fence effortlessly with *The Neon Lounge*, a choreographic work for twelve dancers, set to an existing piece called *Weather* by the New York composer Michael Gordon. Through the dancers she manipulates the space like a true architect, bending diagonals into diamonds, unravelling them to form straight lines, dissolving these little by little and shaping broad semicircles from them. They are then doubled, mirrored and contrasted. She conjures with abstract forms like a contemporary Lev Ivanov. At the same time, a few of the repetitive elements in the choreography are

Photo S. Vanfleteren

reminiscent of minimalist dance. Yet she is not concerned solely with forms and structures. As a child of her time she scatters 'dramatic' elements throughout: sudden eruptions of movement or frozen movements, for example. She thereby breaks down the formality of the choreography. This dynamic, mathematical game is accentuated by the austere set, which comprises panels that frame the space and floating fluorescent tubes that switch from ghostly blue to poisonous green to acacia red: no relaxing lounge atmosphere, nor a trendy disco, but a space packed with physical energy.

The success of Linning's debut on a large stage was honoured by her appointment as the resident choreographer at *Scapino Ballet Rotterdam*. In addition to this she continues to work freelance. A group work commissioned by *Scapino*, called *Scum*, makes it apparent how earnestly this young choreographer is searching. The basis of *Scum* is almost anecdotal. For this piece she worked exclusively with men - nine of them - and made this into its theme. Once again she set the dance in an enclosed space, a bleak underground cellar or car park. In this oppressive, realistic set the men danced with vitality and robustness. The diagonal is like a magic line to which they always returned after solos, duets and trios. The film-like soundtrack by Michiel Jansen - with gunshots and snorting horses - evoked the world of cowboys

THE NEON LOUNGE, 2000

Photo H. Gerritsen

and had a comical effect, as did the pictures from westerns shown on video monitors. The metaphor of the Wild West did not entirely work.

In *Lighthouse*, a group piece, Linning more convincingly achieves a contemporary expressionism. The choreography creates an ominous sensation that is fostered by Ton Bruynèl's driving music. The lighting design also accentuates the grave undertone. A revolving beam of light cuts through the darkness and 'betrays' the dancers' positions. An infra-red camera actually looks right through them. This mysterious and sinister image gives a highly-charged picture of people's vulnerability in an inaccessible world. Consolation is provided by the three solists, however. In ballet shoes and brightly-lit colourful glittery dresses, they look just like radiant angels.

NANINE LINNING
Amsterdam, b. 1977

EDUCATION AND CAREER
Studied at the *Rotterdamse Dansacademie* (specialised in choreography).
Work placement at *Ballett Frankfurt*.

Made her choreographic debut in 1996 (*Metro*).
Since 2002 has been the resident choreographer at *Scapino Ballet Rotterdam* and also works
as a freelance choreographer.

WORKS
Metro, 1996; *Mono / Stereo* (duet Linning / Listopad), 1997; *Skunk, 1997*; *Tribeca*, 1998;
Cardiac Motion, 1999; *Solo*, 1999; *Indecision Ensign* (TWOOLS 1*)*, 1999; *Solo 2.0,* 1999; *Solo
5.0,* 2000; *Anatomism*, 2000; *The Neon Lounge*, 2000; *Loog II* (solo), 2000; *Karpp...?*, 2001;
No Artificial Sweetener (in association with the poet Mustafa Stitou), 2001; *Scum*, 2002;
Lighthouse, 2002

BIBLIOGRAPHY
Ingrid van Frankenhuyzen, 'Er moet mensenvlees in', in *NRC Handelsblad*, 22 September 2000.

FILMS - VIDEOS - TELEVISION RECORDINGS
Solo 5.0, NPS, 2001

ADDRESS
Scapino Ballet Rotterdam, Eendrachtsstraat 8, NL-3012 XL Rotterdam
Tel.: +31 (0)10 414 24 14
Fax: +31 (0)10 413 22 50
info@naninelinning.nl
www.naninelinning.nl

Het Nationale Ballet

Het Nationale Ballet (HNB) is the largest, and the only classical, ballet company in the Netherlands. Its base is at *Het Muziektheater* in Amsterdam, and it has about eighty dancers. This group was set up in 1961 and it performs a wide range of classics from the nineteenth century and the standard international twentieth-century repertoires, as well as new contemporary work.

The romantic classical ballets are by English choreographers (*Giselle*, *The Sleeping Beauty*, *Cinderella*). Cranko's *Onegin* was recently added. Adaptations of *Swan Lake*, *Romeo and Juliet*, *Notenkraker en Muizenkoning* (Nutcracker and Mouse-King) have been made in-house. The twentieth-century repertoire includes ballets from the period of the *Ballets Russes*. A prominent place is taken by the neoclassical work of George Balanchine. Modern work (now historical) by Jerome Robbins and Martha Graham is also danced, as well as ballets by the former resident choreographers Hans van Manen, Toer van Schayk and Rudi van Dantzig.

William Forsythe's *Artifact* is a showpiece when it comes to contemporary ballet. Changes will be taking place at the head of the ballet in June 2003, when Wayne Eagling will be handing the reins over to the Dutchman Ted Brandsen, a choreographer and ex-HNB dancer. He is one of the new generation of choreographers, along with Krzysztof Pastor and David Dawson.

Bibliography

Luuk Utrecht, *Het Nationale Ballet 25 jaar. De geschiedenis van Het Nationale Ballet van 1961 tot 1986*, Uitgeverij Allert de Lange and Het Nationale Ballet, Amsterdam, 1987.

Address

Waterlooplein 22, NL-1011 PG Amsterdam
Tel.: +31 (0)20 551 82 25
Fax: +31 (0)20 551 80 70
info@het-nationale-ballet.nl
www.het-nationale-ballet.nl

NEDERLANDS DANS THEATER

Under the artistic leadership of Jiří Kylián (1975-1999), the *Nederlands Dans Theater* (NDT) has proven itself to be a major contemporary company. The present artistic director is Marian Särstadt, and the business manager is Jaap Hulsman. The company has a worldwide reputation. Choreographers closely associated with it are Jiří Kylián and Hans van Manen. The work of Mats Ek, William Forsythe and Ohad Naharin add various tints to the contemporary repertoire. It is now up to the 'sons of the masters', who include Paul Lightfoot and Sol León, Patrick Delcroix and Johan Inger (already leader of the *Cullberg Ballet*). Since 1988 the company has had a fine home in a theatre designed by the architect Rem Koolhaas in the heart of The Hague. It has the right to first performance.

The NDT1 team comprises 32 dancers, all of whom can call themselves soloists. The youngsters of NDT2 dance the existing repertoire, including works by Kylián. In addition, Paul Lightfoot and others have created pieces specially for their youthful vitality. NDT3, the 'over-40' group, whose core members are Sabine Kupferberg, Egon Madsen, David Krügel, Gioconda Barbito and the guest dancer Gérard Lemaître usually dance in smaller theatres. The work is tailored to their experience of life. The Dutch-Japanese choreographer Shusaku Takeuchi has produced a trilogy for them. NDT3's future is uncertain.

BIBLIOGRAPHY

Coos Versteeg, *Nederlands Dans Theater. Een revolutionaire geschiedenis*, Uitgeverij Balans, Amsterdam, 1987.

ADDRESS

Schedeldoekshaven 60, NL-2511 EN Den Haag
Tel.: +31 (0)70 360 99 31
Fax: +31 (0)70 361 71 56
info@ndt.nl
www.ndt.nl

Korzo Theater

Korzo Theater is a major production center and presentation platform for new and young creators of dance. Over a good ten years, this theatre with its three stages and several studios has acquired a reputation throughout the Netherlands as a place where new and interesting work is to be found. Its programme manager, Leo Spreksel, keeps a close eye on the development of young talent. Bruno Listopad and Paul Selwyn Norton are two who in the meantime have proven their worth. Recent discoveries include André Gingras and the former NDT dancer Dylan Newcomb. After the first two parts of Newcomb's trilogy *FULL CIRCLE*, called *Static* and *Via*, he completed it with *Breath*, and the whole work was the great surprise of the 2001-02 season.

Korzo organises the biennial *CaDance Festival* together with the medium-sized *Theater aan het Spui* in The Hague. *Four Steps Forward* is an opportunity for four choreographers from The Hague to present a short piece. *Voorjaarsontwaken* (Spring Awakening) is an event lasting several days, for choreographers making their debut, including Padma Menon, Ann van de Broek and Jérôme A. Meyer. *Korzo* maintains contacts with *Tanzhaus NRW* in Düsseldorf, which has led to the *Dance Link* exchange project.

Korzo's liveliness - it also programmes theatre and world music - and its system of bringing together creative young people means it can rely on a loyal and involved audience.

Address

Prinsestraat 42, NL-2513 CE Den Haag
Tel.: +31 (0)70 363 75 40
Fax: +31 (0)70 356 22 51
korzo@korzo.nl
www.korzo.nl

Raz

Raz was founded in 1990. Its choreographer Hans Tuerlings creates highly individual dance theatre with a small core of dancers including the actor Karl Schappell, Dina ed Dik, Ulrike Doszmann, Gavin Louis, Susanne Ohmann and Erika Winkler. With irony and a warm compassion he sheds light on our earthly existence in a pithy dance idiom, a restrained and effective set and tightly-reined timing. As a non-dancer and a contrary choreographer Tuerlings often draws his inspiration from outside the world of dance. From 1992 to 1996 his affinity with the French writer Céline inspired him to make the four-part *De reis* (The Journey). In 1997 he started on *Casa del sogno*, based on the names of rooms in the 'dream house' of the extravagant and decadent Italian poet Gabriele d'Annunzio (1863-1938) on Lake Garda. Tuerlings' passion for Italy, the land of art and the good life, is closely related to this series, whose latest parts are *Mappamondo*, *Zambracca* and *Oratorio*.

Hans Tuerlings seeks out and investigates the tension between dance and theatre, anecdote and abstraction. His work is fragmentary in form and makes demands on the spectator's imagination. He calls his individual way of seeing, listening and designing, the 'logic of the dream'. In addition to a dance-theatre piece by Gavin Louis, the *Angelo senza Angelo* programme (2002) includes a striking duet by Tuerlings. He also makes performances for children with the writer Helen Volman and composer Jeroen van Vliet, playful miniature versions of his adult work, such as *Il piccolo David*.

BIBLIOGRAPHY
Het zwarte boekje, Raz, Tilburg, 1995.

ADDRESS
Ringbaan Zuid 251 A, NL-5021 LR Tilburg
Tel.: +31 (0)13 583 59 29
Fax: +31 (0)13 583 59 20
raz@raz.nl
www.raz.nl

HANS HOF ENSEMBLE

The *Hans Hof Ensemble* has made a name for itself in a very short time, not only in the Netherlands but also in Belgium, Germany and Switzerland. Each of the four choreographer-dancers in the group (Andrea Boll, Andreas Denk, Mischa Dullemen and Klaus Jürgens) already had a career behind them when they joined forces as a collective. *Der Lauf der Dinge* (1996) was the overture to hilarious dance works on the theme of expectations that too often turn out to be illusions. Some productions are lighter than others. *Höhenluft* (1998), in which four people meet in a sanatorium, is mainly comical, while *Stad bij nacht* (City at Night, 1999), about anonymity in the metropolis, is somewhat more serious. But all their productions are made on the basis of a certain sense of melancholy and they also like to play with clichés. *Geluk* (Happiness, 2001) is a tragi-comic sketch of the way every one of us searches for happiness. The eye-catcher is Edwin Kopla's set, a jungle of artificial plants like a plastic Garden of Eden. Yet in bursts it is also both poetic and moving.

The group inhabits the territory somewhere between Bausch and Vandekeybus. It displays virtuosity in its acting and group passages and inventiveness in the use of props. The key to this is perfect timing, as demonstrated by Andreas Denk in *Sophie*. Their work is not too light. The absurd jokes have a critical undertone (*Bureau*, 2002).

ADDRESS

Entrepotdok 4, NL-1018 AD Amsterdam
Tel.: +31 (0)20 627 65 82
Fax: +31 (0)20 638 22 65
info@hanshof.nl
www.hanshof.nl

INTRODANS

Introdans is a company of about 30 dancers. Its artistic leaders are Ton Wiggers and Roel Voorintholt. Its business manager is Johan Taal. Its repertoire is varied and comprises contemporary music ballets by Nils Christe, modern dance by Conny Janssen and dance theatre by the Finnish choreographer Jorma Uotinen.

Introdans also dances adaptations of the classics, including pieces by the Spanish Ramón Oller, *Romy & July* and *La fille mal gardée*, and by the French Maryse Delente, *Giselle of de romantische leugen* (Giselle or the Romantic Lie). Apart from these modern-style narrative ballets, they present triple bill programmes on a theme, such as *Klassiekers in Muziek en dans* (Classics of Music and Dance).

A great deal of care is put into their design, and the costumes have a modern cut. The dancers are of many nationalities and all have a classical background, which they combine with a modern dynamism and charisma.

2001 saw the group's 30th anniversary (Hans Focking, one of the co-founders, has already retired) and can look back on a successful development from a regional amenity to a company that operates nationwide. In recent years its leaders have also looked abroad, specifically to the German state of Nordrhein-Westfalen. The success of *Introdans. Ensemble voor de Jeugd* (Youth Ensemble) led by Roel Voorintholt even extends as far as New York and Asia.

BIBLIOGRAPHY
Ine Rietstap and Marian van Hooij, *Introdans – dertig jaar passie voor de dans 1971-2001*, Introdans, Arnhem, 2001.

ADDRESS
Vijfzinnenstraat 80-82, NL-6811 LN Arnhem
Tel.: +31 (0)26 251 21 11
Fax: +31 (0)26 351 56 47
welcome@introdans.nl
www.introdans.nl

INTRODANS. ENSEMBLE VOOR DE JEUGD
MEEKERS
DANSTHEATER AYA

The Netherlands has a tradition of dance for young people. *Scapino Ballet* was established as early as 1945. The diversity of contemporary dance is reflected in the dance that is created for the young.

Introdans is a company that presents dance both for adults and for the young. The youth ensemble, headed by Roel Voorintholt, puts on full-length programmes on connective themes, as in *Mmmozart*, which was compiled from pieces by Hans van Manen and Patrick Delcroix, among others. The company also performs contemporary adaptations of narrative ballets (*Giselle & Co.* by Maryse Delente and Ton Wiggers) and of well-known works of children's literature such as *Pinokkio* (Karole Armitage).

The style Arthur Rosenfeld of *Meekers* uses in his work for children is not essentially different from that in his 'adult' pieces. His dance theatre is associative in form and is composed flexibly around a theme, such as history in the case of *En toch beweegt het!* (But It Does Move!). Humour is a constant ingredient. His work is playful and deliberately not educational, and appeals to the heart and the mind.

By contrast, Wies Bloemen of *Danstheater Aya* makes full use of the experiences and feelings of teenagers. She goes into such topics as being in love in *Bronsttijd* (The Mating Season), violence, rage and powerlessness in *Drijfzand* (Quicksand) and the animal nature of man in *Beest* (Beast). *Danstheater Aya* is popular among youngsters because of its trendy approach, with hiphop and skate-dance.

BIBLIOGRAPHY

De schatkist van de dans – 10 jaar Introdans. Ensemble voor de jeugd, Introdans, Arnhem, 1999.

ADDRESSES

Introdans. Ensemble voor de jeugd
Vijfzinnenstraat 80-82, NL-6811 LN Arnhem
Tel.: +31 (0)26 251 21 11
Fax: +31 (0)26 351 56 47
welcome@introdans.nl
www.introdans.nl

Meekers
Coolhaven 96 - 98, NL-3024 AG Rotterdam
Tel.: +31 (0)10 244 98 93
Fax: +31 (0)10 244 98 94
info@meekers.nl
www.meekers.nl

Danstheater Aya
Contactweg 42 H, NL-1014 AN Amsterdam
Tel.: +31 (0)20 386 85 74
Fax: +31 (0)20 486 86 80
info@aya.nl
www.aya.nl

DansWerkplaats Amsterdam
Dansateliers Rotterdam

DansWerkplaats Amsterdam (DWA), led by Ger Jager since it was founded in 1993, provides new choreographers with artistic, business and service support. They are given space for their explorations and are able to present their very first work in the privacy of the studio theatre. An exchange system with other workshops and / or production companies makes it possible to organise short tours of the Netherlands. Performances are also put on in such theatres as *Korzo* in The Hague and the *NES Theaters* in Amsterdam.

Choreographers who have made successful presentations include Uri Ivgi, Jean-Louis Barning, Sara Wookey, Sarah van Lamsweerde and Marc Nukoop. Among others whose turn it has recently been are Marc van Loon, Nora Heilmann, Annabelle López Ochoa, Kenzo Kusuda and Troy Mundy. There are links with the *School voor Nieuwe Dans Ontwikkelingen* in Amsterdam, but they are not exclusive.

Ex-dancers from major companies can also apply to DWA. There is no collective artistic name, but everyone contributes to contemporary dance on the basis of their background and experience. DWA has initiated *Aerodance*, an exchange programme for young European choreographers, which is part of *Julidans*. In 2002 DWA appeared at the *Oerol* festival on Terschelling.

A second workshop with an established reputation is the *Dansateliers Rotterdam*, headed by the former dancer and choreographer Amy Gale. This is a true laboratory where creative young people can complete short projects and be assured of critical artistic feedback.

Addresses
DansWerkplaats Amsterdam
Arie Biemondstraat 107 B, NL-1054 PD Amsterdam
Tel.: +31 (0)20 689 17 89
Fax: +31 (0)20 612 43 24
info.dwa@euronet.nl
www.euronet.nl/~dwa

Dansateliers Rotterdam
's-Gravendijkwal 58 B, NL-3014 EE Rotterdam
Tel.: +31 (0)10 436 99 37
Fax: +31 (0)10 436 09 15
info@dansateliers.nl

HOLLAND DANCE FESTIVAL
SPRINGDANCE
JULIDANS

The *Holland Dance Festival* (HDF) is the most important international dance event in the Netherlands. This biennial operates at a European level. Its artistic director, Samuel Wuersten, presents a varied package of international dance trends from the 'middle circuit' - between the small-scale avant-garde and the established companies. It is a tradition that the *Nederlands Dans Theater* takes part in the HDF. Four theatres join in and it is no exaggeration to say that during this event 'The Hague dances'. Previous themes of the festival have been 'the freelancer as entrepreneur and co-author', 'dance and health' and 'non-western dance and ballet'. One of its constant aims is to present exceptional performances, such as Mikhail Baryshnikov's first appearance in the Netherlands.

Alternating with HDF, *Springdance* is also held biennially in Utrecht. The two of them cohabit very easily. With the appointment of Simon Dove as its director *Springdance* turns in the direction of neoconceptual dance, and a series of young Europeans has been introduced. This platform for international contemporary dance is accompanied by additional activities such as *Preview*, for young performers, and *Dialogue*, a first step towards a critical debate between the artists and the audience.

Julidans was initiated in 1991 as the summer programme of the *Stadsschouwburg* in Amsterdam, but it has expanded into a successful annual festival in its own right. It programmes contemporary dance with a theatrical appeal.

ADDRESSES
Holland Dance Festival
Nobelstraat 21, NL-2513 BC Den Haag
Tel.: +31 (0)70 361 61 42
Fax: +31 (0)70 365 05 09
info@hollanddancefestival.com
www.hollanddancefestival.com

Springdance
Postbus 111, NL-3500 AC Utrecht
Tel.: +31 (0)30 233 20 32
Fax: +31 (0)30 230 38 81
mail@springdance.nl
www.springdance.nl

Julidans
Stadsschouwburg Amsterdam
Leidseplein 26, NL-1017 PT Amsterdam
Tel.: +31 (0)20 523 77 70
Fax: +31 (0)20 623 86 85
julidans@stadsschouwburgamsterdam.nl
www.julidans.com

REINVENTING DANCE OVER AND OVER AGAIN

Art never just bubbles up from nowhere. But the wave of dazzling dance innovation that broke in Belgium in the early 1980s had not been in the least predicted or expected. It seemed like a guerilla invasion by a handful of performing artists run wild. Their revolutionary message could not have come at a better time. Running radically counter to the established customs of the 'ballet' world - which looked on with suspicion and incomprehension - this young movement reached an eager new dance audience. Because once the fuse had been lit, more and more young hotheads kept on emerging, like Resistance fighters, from dark rehearsal rooms, squatters' houses, musty warehouses and chilly lofts. All with their own diverse and highly individual ideas about what dance might mean to them. Their weapons, devised and refined in secret over the years, were now put into action, roughly, with no frills, but keenly and effectively. No one could afford professional dancers, and the quality of the performance often left a lot to be desired, but the artistic statements were overwhelming and convincing. The insights gained in dance and other disciplines by American postmodernism, which at that time was already past its peak, had hardly penetrated into Belgium. The principle of 'anything is possible' was reinvented on the spot and, in all innocence (or not), applied in a totally self-willed way. There were no rules, and no one worried about style or proper composition; no one wondered whether the result was truly dance or not.

It soon turned out that the notion of 'dance' was due for redefinition. Structuralism and chaos were set shamelessly alongside each other and when they met sparks flew. The borders with theatre and the other arts were cautiously probed or unhesitatingly overstepped: dance theatre was given new meaning and came closer to being an all-embracing art form. The space, manipulated or otherwise, was given a value equal to what took place in it; film and video were not the set or an illustration, but an artistic and sometimes independent element. The exploration and expression of emotions was expanded and explored. Dancers descended into the catacombs of the body, looking for indefinable sources, resulting in even more extreme physical developments: from fiery, frenetic dynamism to rarefied, agonising slowness. Attention was also paid to common-sense constructivism, the cosmic and the spiritual. Irony and cynicism, stark earnestness and relativising nonchalance, beauty and anti-beauty all encountered each other in twilight zones and created an oddly poetic atmosphere or an indefinable tension. The astonished audiences let themselves be carried along in this enthralling adventure. In just a few years, the combatants from the opening bouts had enthusiastic followers throughout the world. Brussels took over from New York as the place to be, the new Mecca of dance.

Yet Belgium had never had a real dance tradition. It is true that in 1826 Antoine Petipa founded a dance academy at the *Muntschouwburg* in Brussels, and a ballet group was established at the opera in Ghent in 1841, but at the *Koninklijke Opera van Antwerpen* (Royal Opera of Antwerp), founded in 1893, the dance passages were deleted from the score because there was no dance company. Between the wars (1918-1940) the opera ballet groups in Antwerp, Ghent and Brussels continued to provide the *divertimenti* in opera productions, but a number of extraordinary teachers also appeared, followers of the Eastern European *Ausdruckstanz*, who propagated the view of dance as an independent modern art form: Lea Daan, Isa Voss and Elsa Darciel. However, it was the Brabants sisters, who had drunk at the well of German expressionist dance, who created professional structures for dance in Antwerp after World War II.

In Brussels, a singular art deco dance artist called Akarova was a hit in

Julio Arozarena in Danny Rosseel's *Spent Passions*,
Koninklijk Ballet van Vlaanderen, 1992 (Photo P. de Backer)

A. Prokovsky's *De notenkraker* (The Nutcracker),
Koninklijk Ballet van Vlaanderen, 1997 (Photo P. de Backer)

intellectual circles. She was not unacquainted with the teachings of Rudolf Laban, but she drew the bulk of her inspiration from Raymond Duncan, the eccentric brother of Isadora Duncan. But he danced without music, whereas Akarova, who had had musical training, found music essential to her dance inspiration. One of the foremost art deco designers of the time, her husband Marcel Baugniet, designed unforgettable geometric sets and costumes for her performances. But the constructivist costumes that Akarova drew for herself still make a powerful impression today. In her dance movements she sought the angularity of art deco, and the rhythms were inspired by those of machines and mechanical operations. The result was a dramatically-charged but also visually intense geometric dance which was clearly well ahead of its time. She learnt the creative use of lighting from the theatre innovator Herman Teirlinck, who invited her to take part in the theatre experiments he was leading at the *La Cambre* school, whose head was Henry van de Velde. She later employed these techniques in the small art deco theatre she had built in Brussels, where she organised music recitals and performances by dance and theatre companies. Despite her frequent contacts with foreign artists, Akarova's appeal did not extend abroad, and what is worse she passed into obscurity in her own country too. Until 1988, that is, when the *Fondation pour l'architecture* in Brussels rehabilitated her in an exhibition of costumes and sets and the publication of a hefty volume.

Béjart in Brussels

After World War II Jeanne Brabants, founder and inspirer of the Antwerp ballet school and the *Koninklijk Ballet van Vlaanderen* (Royal Flanders Ballet), struggled unflaggingly for the official recognition of dance as a proper artistic medium.

However, it was actually a foreigner who aroused the love of dance in the public at large. In 1959 the French choreographer Maurice Béjart was invited to head the ballet company at the Brussels opera house, *De Munt*. He accepted on condition that it would become an independent company free of the obligation to provide the opera *divertimenti*. Béjart gave the conservative classical ballet audience a good shake-up with movements that broke away from the normal vocabulary of dance: decentralised hips, back undulations and contractions, which he derived from Indian and African dance, jazz dance and disco. He took a young intellectual audience by surprise with brilliantly choreographed ballets such as *Le Sacre du printemps* and *Boléro* and for more than a quarter of a century his *Ballet van de XXste Eeuw* (Ballet of the 20th Century) threw packed sports stadiums into raptures (ordinary theatres were too small!) all over the world. At *Mudra*, the school he founded, he wanted to train a new sort of dance artist. The curriculum included yoga and theatre alongside musical analysis and the more usual subjects. *Mudra* became one of the most important innovative dance courses in Europe and produced numerous exciting dancers and choreographers such as Maguy Marin, Nicole Mossoux, Anne Teresa de Keersmaeker, Michèle-Anne de Mey and Pierre Droulers.

Until the eighties, Béjart counted as one of the most interesting postwar European dance innovators. So great was his impact that after almost twenty years, still hardly anyone dared vie with him. There was virtually no interest in innovative dance companies from abroad either. The whole American postmodern dance movement, which developed in exactly the same period, passed Europe by almost unnoticed, and Belgium certainly.

This began to change in 1980. The Béjart mania started to wane and there was growing curiosity about new forms of dance. In 1987 disagreements between Béjart and the director of *De Munt*, Gerard Mortier, led to a parting of the ways. Béjart left for Lausanne, where he worked on the next stage of his career. A year later the

Maurice Béjart's *Les Illuminations*, 1979
(De Munt archives, Brussels / Photo A. Béjart)

Maurice Béjart's *Le Sacre du printemps*, 1984
(De Munt archives, Brussels / Photo W. Dupont)

Mudra school closed, despite the forceful protests of Jeanne Brabants, who considered the continued existence of *Mudra* to be of crucial importance, both artistically and financially. After all, when it closed, the subsidies went too. Brabants was soon proved right. Less than ten years later Brussels was once more a flourishing centre of dance, but mostly with foreign dancers working for Belgian companies. This was a heavy administrative and financial burden, however. Anne Teresa de Keersmaeker, who had now become the resident choreographer at *De Munt* after the American choreographer Mark Morris had spent a short time in the post, acted on an urgent need. She founded a new 'school' on the lines of *Mudra*, though the word 'school' is a rather stuffy one for the artistic concept behind this course. *PARTS* stands for *Performing Arts Research and Training Studios*. Just like *Mudra*, musical analysis is taught alongside the most diverse contemporary dance lessons (a substantial part of which is reserved for contemporary-classical ballet technique). For this musical analysis, De Keersmaeker originally invited the legendary, but now deceased Fernand Schirren, her former teacher at *Mudra* to whom she owed many of her own musical insights. Theoretical lessons such as art philosophy and dance history play an important part in preparing young artists intellectually for their creative tasks.

Young and Wild
When the young Anne Teresa de Keersmaeker returned from a short period of study in New York in 1982, bringing back her minimalist piece *Fase, Four Movements to the Music of Steve Reich*, this production was the explosion that signalled a new revolutionary era.

In the same year, the Antwerp artist Jan Fabre caused a sensation with his eight-hour piece *Het is theater zoals te verwachten en te voorzien was* (It is Theatre as was to be Expected and Foreseen). This work abstracted such emotional elements as aggression, pain, suffering and exhaustion in such a way, free of any narrative context and set in an extremely powerful visually orchestrated series of evolving images, that it could be read as a dance performance. Fabre, a graphic artist by training, had also spent a few years in New York, where he had laid the foundations of his performance art. A new age had dawned. The success of these two artists had the effect of an infectious virus. The content of their work initially referred very much to American postmodernism and generated a sudden and substantial interest in that movement. The *Kaaitheater* and *Théâtre 140* in Brussels had been sporadically inviting foreign avant-garde theatre and dance artists for a while. In 1983 the *Klapstuk* dance festival was launched in Leuven, a true biennial of contemporary dance. Under the leadership of Michel Uytterhoeven, this festival brought the leading figures of American postmodernism to Belgium: Lucinda Childs, Trisha Brown and Steve Paxton. They were later followed by young dance artists from France, Spain, Portugal, the former Yugoslavia, Japan (bringing the revelation of *butoh*) and Belgium. This was because young choreographers all over the country were suddenly demanding that attention be paid to their very new and fragile works, full of imperfections (technical and otherwise) but also keen, radically innovative ideas. It seemed that in their unstoppable urge to create there was no time left to become technically competent first. Anyway, the traditional techniques of dance and choreography were not capable of giving shape to this huge variety of fantasies. The public seemed to be so enraptured by the concept that the variable quality of the performance was happily accepted as charming and only a side issue. The motto was: rather enthralling content with a shaky form than a perfectly rounded form with a boring message.

Mark Morris's *The Hard Nut*, De Munt, 1991 (Photo T. Brazil)

Springboards

To cater for the needs of all this youthful enthusiasm, Herbert Reymer and a small group of staff set up a festival called *De Beweeging* in Antwerp in 1984. It was biennial and operated on extremely limited funds, but provided new artists of movement with what they most needed: a stage and an inquisitive, adventurous audience, and, later, encounters with young foreign choreographers too.

De Beweeging was the springboard for many Belgian choreographers, and frequently led to their performing abroad too (this was not true of De Keersmaeker and Fabre, who by that time were already in the international circuit, or Wim Vandekeybus, who in 1987 took off like a rocket straight onto the international scene). Alain Platel soon appeared with his acute observations on, and his warm, generous love for, the bizarre, petty, sometimes psychotic sides of our fellow humans and ourselves, in such moving, odd pieces as *Stabat Mater* and *Mange P'tit Coucou*. The works that Nicole Mossoux and Patrick Bonté meticulously and sublimely created were equally bizarre, but rather surrealistic, mythical pieces of dance poetry. Marc Vanrunxt sees the study of the movement itself as a metaphor for the possibilities and impossibilities of movement in life, and the study of beauty as a subtle symbiosis of exuberant kitsch and restrained minimalism, chaos as another structural order, and *vice versa*. Eric Raeves, one of Vanrunxt's associates from the very beginning and always closely involved in the creation of his extravagant costumes, emerged as a master in the creation of *tableaux vivants*. The choreographic work of José Besprosvany, a Mexican who stayed on in Brussels after his training at *Mudra*, developed from a powerfully repetitive minimalism to a dance theatre with a strong, highly individual idiom of movement. Bert van Gorp disarms his confreres' intellectualism with boyish mischievousness and comical *camp* (homosexual) kitsch. This also counteracts the sensually erotic works by Thierry Smits, who has developed a stylised dance idiom that is like a continuation of the renewal of the classical ballet idiom that Béjart had set in motion, and who also has an acute aesthetic sense and soon gathered a considerable following.

Many took their first steps at *De Beweeging*. But however fascinating and however obstinately it pressed on, this new dance nevertheless only took off very laboriously. The first performances were usually achieved by means of private and therefore very modest means; a source that is of course soon exhausted. There were hardly any subsidies or other backing to set up dance productions under normal professional conditions. Theatres and cultural centres were sporadically willing to use high-risk budgets to put on a contemporary dance performance. Initiatives such as *vzw Schaamte* were few and far between. This collective, founded by Hugo de Greef, assembled a variety of promising young theatre and dance people under one roof. A single administrative service, infrastructure and promotional system were shared by all the performers involved. All their income also went into a single kitty. So anyone who earned a lot supported the others. But those who were strong enough to take off on their own were encouraged to leave the nest. This enabled performing artists like Jan Lauwers, Josse de Pauw, Jan de Corte and Anne Teresa de Keersmaeker to spread their wings. This method was also employed later by Alain Platel when he set young colleagues to work in his *Ballets C de la B* so that their work could mature under the secure wing of a company which, already having state support, was able to look after the administrative and promotional side of things and guarantee artistic guidance. Other companies whose operations were recognised and subsidised later followed this example.

The Belgian Rift

For a long time the government continued to take the advice of the representatives of classical ballet: all this wild young activity was dismissed as being neither dance nor art. Attitudes to this new dance gradually became more charitable. But in

Jan Fabre's *De danssecties* (The Dance Sections), 1987 (Photo J. Fabre)

Anne Teresa de Keersmaeker and Michèle-Anne de Mey,
scène from Thierry de Mey's film *Fase*, 2002

Belgium the government is divided. There are three language communities (the Flemish Community, the French Community, and the German-speaking Community) and three regions (Flanders, Wallonia and Brussels). In addition, the Brussels Region has individual status. Culture is a matter for the communities. But there are also 'Belgian' national institutions. This means that when it comes to culture, decisions are made at various levels.

Here are a few examples. After the death of Jorge Lefevre, the director of the *Ballet royal de Wallonie*, the French Community decided to transform the company, which was based in the impoverished Walloon industrial city of Charleroi, into a *Centre chorégraphique de la Communauté française*. Led by Frédéric Flamand, who merged the centre with his own *Plan K* company, this soon became a flamboyant location where contemporary dance was created and shown. In the 1990s *Charleroi Danses* became a familiar concept. The opera house in Brussels, *De Munt*, is a federal 'Belgian' institution, whereas Rosas, Anne Teresa de Keersmaeker's company that is in residence there, receives subsidies from the Flemish Community. Such situations sometimes make cultural life extremely complex. A 'Flemish' choreographer with a 'French' administrator and dancers who originate from all over the world, can in theory choose which authorities he requests subsidies from. In this way, a Dutch-speaking choreographer like Thierry Smits is subsidised by the French Community, but he nevertheless has an audience among the Flemish public. As a result of their forceful initiatives, performers, programme makers, theatre and festival organisers have often faced the authorities with a *fait accompli*, so that projects and subsidies have gradually been made possible across the dividing lines. Yet *Contredanse*, a French Community organisation for information on dance, and the *Vlaams Theater Instituut* (Flemish Theatre Institute), both indispensable to the Belgian dance scene, continue to function separately, just a stone's throw from each other.

The complex Belgian situation has its effect on this book too. A great many Belgian choreographers, especially from Brussels, will not appear here. In any case, this publication offers only an outline of the many sides of the art of movement that can be seen in Brussels and Flanders.

Better Support

In 1993, advisory boards were set up to assist the Flemish Community's Ministry of Culture. The first advisory board for dance was immediately able to persuade the minister that contemporary dance was in urgent need of better support. At that time, such choreographers as Anne Teresa de Keersmaeker, Jan Fabre, Wim Vandekeybus and Alain Platel were on the bill at the most important theatres and the most controversial festivals around the world, and they were also being awarded prestigious prizes. In short, the international dance world was talking with great respect of 'the Belgian Boom' and 'the Flemish Wave'. Whole festivals were even devoted to it. Brussels had become the place to be for contemporary dance. Yet these heroes of Flemish dance still had to work in wretched conditions. Production funding depended on backing from a theatre, a workshop or a production company, and were therefore extremely insecure. The dancers, and often the choreographer and the leaders of the company too, often had to rely on unemployment benefit and various schemes by which they could work and be paid by the state (though with no rights) and were not able to fall back on social security. At that time most of the productions by the 'well-known' choreographers were produced with financial backing from theatres and festivals abroad, and they had offers to move into residence in major theatres elsewhere in the world. If these valuable performing artists were not to be lost, a price had to be paid. Moves were undertaken to make up for lost ground in contemporary dance by increasing the budgets bit by bit (the total sum of which still came nowhere near what the *Koninklijk Ballet van*

Annamirl van der Pluym in *Solo M*, 1994 (Photo M. Pellanders / Hollandse Hoogte)

Vlaanderen alone received) and initiatives introduced that resulted in, among other things, a better social status for dancers. An improved subsidy policy also led to better and higher-quality productions, which in their turn were accepted more easily by theatres and were made more accessible to the public. Supply and demand became better geared to each other.

Hothouse Brussels

Since *PARTS* was set up, many of its students have stayed on in Brussels, precisely because it is such an artistic hothouse. Some of them have successfully entered the professional dance scene, and this does not apply only to *PARTS* students. Young talent has also made its appearance under the wings of Jan Fabre, Wim Vandekeybus, Alain Platel and Michèle-Anne de Mey, among others, and the *Hoger Instituut voor Dans* (Higher Institute for Dance) in Lier - Antwerp. And these people enter the profession with both a thoroughly-learnt dance technique and a sound theoretical background. The discourse they are now setting out is of a completely different order from that of twenty years ago, but just as exciting. And once again a young intellectual public is being won over and swept along.

The internationalisation of the people involved in dance, and the openness to other cultures, as well as the will not to become stuck in idioms (old or new) and the conviction of the importance of artistic, intellectual and technical flexibility are also leading to the growth of new trends. Nowadays, breakdancers share the stage with flamenco dancers, belly dancers, Indian dancers and classical dansers, contemporary dancers and ballerinas. These encounters lead to flamboyant clashes and dazzling explosions, but also to beautiful symbiotic works of dance. The potential is far from exhausted. The fact that in 2002 the first contemporary dance artist, Jan Fabre, is doing a production with the *Koninklijk Ballet van Vlaanderen* (and of no less than *Swan Lake!*) is clearly another step in the direction of a new openness, tolerance and mutual artistic appreciation.

BIBLIOGRAPHY

MAURICE BÉJART, Un instant dans la vie d'autrui, Flammarion, Paris, 1979.

'Danse en Flandre', in *Danser maintenant*, CFC Éditions, Brussels, 1990.

KATIE VERSTOCKT, 'Een storm in een glas water of een nieuw elan voor de dans? Jonge Vlaamse choreografen', in *Ons Erfdeel*, XXXIV, 1991, no. 4, pp. 555-562.

KATIE VERSTOCKT, 'La danse contemporaine en Flandre', in *Septentrion, revue de culture néerlandaise*, XXI, 1992, no. 4, pp. 27-32.

AN-MARIE LAMBRECHTS, MARIANNE VAN KERKHOVEN and KATIE VERSTOCKT (eds.), *Dans in Vlaanderen*, Stichting Kunstboek, Bruges, 1996.

AN-MARIE LAMBRECHTS, MARIANNE VAN KERKHOVEN and KATIE VERSTOCKT (eds.), *Dance in Flanders*, Stichting Kunstboek, Bruges, 1996.

JO DEKMINE (ed.), *België. Bakermat van de dans – La Belgique. Refuge de la dance – Belgium. A Sanctuary for Dance – Belgien. Zufluchtsort für den Tanz*, Vlaams Theater Instituut – Charleroi Danses, Brussels - Charleroi, 2000.

PIETER T'JONCK, 'A Seething Cauldron. Dance in Brussels', in *The Low Countries. Arts and Society in Flanders and the Netherlands*, X, 2002, pp. 120-125.

Articles. Promotion Magazine on Dance in Flanders – Magazine de promotion de la dance en Flandre, Vlaams Theater Instituut, Brussels.

NDD – L'actualité de la danse, Contredance asbl, Brussels.

Nouvelles de danse, revue trimestrielle, Contredance asbl, Brussels.

www.vti.be

Jan Fabre

Jan Fabre is a versatile artist. At the heart of his oeuvre lies his visual work, such as the well-known blue ballpoint-covered cloths and installations and his scarab sculptures. He made his definitive breakthrough in the performing arts with his eight-hour performance marathon *Het is theater zoals het te verwachten en te voorzien was* (1982). The physical body already occupied an important place in this early work. Fabre always seeks out the boundaries of what the body can endure. He goes to the limits of exhaustion and creates theatrical situations of menace and unease. He achieves the latter by, among other things, using live animals (including snakes, beetles and birds of prey) in his stage settings. In one of the main scenes in *Het is theater...*, two performers, while jogging, endlessly perform the routine daily actions of getting up, having breakfast and going to work. In counterpoint to this senseless human struggle, Fabre creates the poetic image of several candles moving agonizingly slowly across the stage on the backs of live tortoises.

From 1987, for the movement sequences in his opera trilogy *The Minds of Helena Troubleyn*, which he created with the Polish composer Eugeniusz Knapik, Fabre explored the vocabulary of classical ballet.

Three of his first four choreographic works were directly linked to the opera trilogy. The 1987 *Das Glas im Kopf wird vom Glas. De danssecties* (The Dance Sections) was a preliminary study for the dance material in the first part of the trilogy, of the same name, which only premièred three years later. Fabre here discovered the power of the classical ballet idiom, which he refined even more in a rigidly synchronised, extremely slow-moving minimalist and static movement in which the *'corps de ballet'* was given the role of the star dancer. The degree of physical difficulty and the strict discipline were intensified even more by the fact that in the first part the dancers had to endure wearing a suit of armour. This inspired Fabre to later call his dancers and actors 'warriors of beauty'.

In *The Sound of One Hand Clapping* (1990), created for William Forsythe's *Ballett Frankfurt*, he developed this use of classical ballet poses even further. This ballet was once again a preliminary study for the second part of the opera trilogy, *Silent Screams, Difficult Dreams* (1992). His 1993 choreographic commission for *Het Nationale Ballet* in the Netherlands was also connected to the world of mythical stories that grew up around the fictional opera character Helena Troubleyn. In *Quando la terra si rimette in movimento* (1995), Fabre repeated not only the first line of the libretto of *Das Glas im Kopf* but also its formal elements (the vocabulary of classical ballet, the geometric spatial structures), its design (the use of monumental backcloths) and the colour symbolism, with the ballpoint-blue dream world in which the classical ideal of order and beauty was aspired to, contrasting sharply with the black, chaotic animal underworld.

This contrast between order and chaos, day and night, man and animal is also the main theme of Fabre's most independent and highly developed choreography, *Da un'altra faccia del tempo* (1993). It is composed in three sections, and the order and symmetry of the first transforms into the utter chaos of the infernal second. After this, in a sublime closing image, hundreds of plates and shards fall to the floor and then, amidst the rubble and dust, three ballerinas again perform the familiar strict movements that are Fabre's choreographic trade mark.

Photo S. Vanfleteren

In *Drie solo's* (1995), Fabre refers for the last time to his earlier dance work. To music by Knapik, performed live, the three main dancers, Renée Copraij, Emio Greco and Valerie Valentin repeat their movements from the group choreographic pieces, but now as soloists in the immense emptiness of the stage, bounded only by the monumental cloths in their archetypal colours.

Fabre is always able to surround himself with strong personalities who, in addition to their work with him, also develop an artistic course of their own: Emio Greco, Eric Raeves, Maria Voortman and Roberto de Jonge, Renée Copraij, Wim Vandekeybus, Annamirl van der Pluym and Marc Vanrunxt were all among the first generation of Fabre performers. In 1997 Fabre created a solo for each of the last four, related to and as a tribute to their own artistic personality.

In his most recent work, Fabre has on the one hand returned to the primitive primal force of his very first performances and on the other, with his version of *Swan Lake*, is working on his first classical ballet performance. In *As Long as the World Needs a Warrior's Soul* (2000), a new generation of talented performers explored the limits of their 'own bodies in revolt'. Driven by energetic rock music, they performed instinctive physical rituals in which, for example, they smeared themselves with foodstuffs. Dario Fo's piece on the resistance of the terrorist Ulrike Meinhof was

**THE SOUND OF ONE
HAND CLAPPING, 1990**

Photo D. Mentzos

translated in extreme and physical terms into a woman's labour pains. Destruction and creation are essential complements. In parallel with this group piece, Fabre created a solo for the Icelandic dancer Erna Omarsdottir, who was a graduate of *PARTS*. The instinctive animal language of the human body was also central to *My Movements Are Alone Like Streetdogs* (2001). In contrast to this 'primitive' language, in *Het Zwanenmeer* (2002), created for the *Ballet van Vlaanderen*, he again put the highly disciplined and synchronised ballet idiom into a stylised mythical portrayal of the same basic theme: Eros versus Thanatos.

JAN FABRE

Antwerp, b. 1958

EDUCATION AND CAREER

Studied at the *Stedelijk Instituut voor Sierkunsten en Ambachten* (Antwerp) and the *Koninklijke Academie voor Schone Kunsten* (Antwerp).

In 1986 founded *Troubleyn* (a consistent group of staff for Fabre's various projects).

WORKS

Theater geschreven met een K is een kater, 1980; *Het is theater zoals te verwachten en te voorzien was,* 1982; *De macht der theaterlijke dwaasheden,* 1984; *Das Glas im Kopf wird vom Glas. De danssecties,* 1987; *Prometheus Landschaft,* 1988; *Das Interview das stirbt,* 1988; *Das Glas im Kopf wird vom Glas,* 1990; *The Sound of One Hand Clapping* (for Ballett Frankfurt), 1990; *Sweet Temptations,* 1991; *Wie spreekt mijn gedachte...,* 1992; *Silent Screams, Difficult Dreams,* 1992; *Da un 'altra faccia del tempo,* 1993; *Quando la terra si remette in movimento,* 1995; *Drie solo's,* 1995; *De Vier temperamenten,* 1997: *The Very Seat of Honour* (for Renée Copraij), *Body, Body on the Wall* (for Wim Vandekeybus), *The Pickwick Man* (for Marc Vanrunxt), *Ik ben jaloers op elke zee* (for Annamirl van der Pluym); *My Movemens Are Alone Like Streetdogs* (for Erna Omarsdottir), 2000; *As Long as the World Needs a Warrior's Soul,* 2000; *Het Zwanenmeer* (for the *Ballet van Vlaanderen*), 2002; *Parrots and Guinea Pigs,* 2002

BIBLIOGRAPHY

Stefan Hertmans, 'Jeuk aan de ziel', in *De Gids,* October-November 1992.

Sigrid Bousset (ed.), *Jan Fabre. Texts on his Theatre-Work,* Kaaitheater, Brussels, 1993.

Sigrid Bousset, *Mestkever van de verbeelding. Over Jan Fabre,* De Bezige Bij, Amsterdam, 1994.

Paul Demets, 'Uitdijende ruimte, splijtende tijd: het werk van Jan Fabre', in *Ons Erfdeel,* XXXVII, 1994, no. 5, pp. 643-660.

Emil Hrvatin, *Jan Fabre, la Discipline du chaos, le chaos de la discipline,* Armand Colin, Seine Saint-Denis, 1994.

Emil Hrvatin, *Herhaling, waanzin, discipline. Het theaterwerk van Jan Fabre,* Theatre and Film Books / Kritak, Amsterdam / Leuven, 1994.

A. Wesemann (ed.), *Jan Fabre,* Fischer Taschenbuch Verlag, Frankfurt am Main, 1994.

Hugo de Greef & Jan Hoet, *Gesprekken met Jan Fabre,* De Bezige Bij / Kritak, Amsterdam / Leuven, 1995.

Paul Demets, 'A General of Beauty. The Work of Jan Fabre', in *The Low Countries. Arts and Society in Flanders and the Netherlands,* III, 1995-1996, pp. 117-125.

'Jan Fabre', *Portretten van podiumkunstenaars – Kritisch Theater Lexicon,* Vlaams Theater Instituut, Brussels, 1997 (also in English).

Theatre issue on Jan Fabre, Oscar van Woensel and Jan Lauwers: *De Brakke Hond,* no. 55, 1997.

Emil Hrvatin, *Ripetizione, follia, disciplina. L'opera teatrale di Jan Fabre,* Infinito Ltd, Turin, 2001.

FILMS - VIDEOS - TELEVISION RECORDINGS

Prometheus Landschaft, Kunstkanaal, 1988; *Body, Body on the Wall,* De filmfabriek, 1997; *Les guerriers,* Regard Productions / Periscope Productions, 2002

ADDRESS

Troubleyn, Italiëlei 56, B-2000 Antwerpen
Tel.: +32 (0)3 201 13 00
.Fax: +32 (0)3 233 15 01
anja.delannoy@troubleyn.be   www.troubleyn.be

In 1982 Anne Teresa de Keersmaeker, who had studied at the *Mudra* school under Maurice Béjart, returned to Belgium from New York. She had up her sleeve a performance in the minimalist style, called *Fase, Four Movements to the Music of Steve Reich*. Like Reich's music, she employed repetition and phrasing to develop clear, geometric dance structures. When it opened at the *Beursschouwburg* in Brussels, with herself and Michèle-Anne de Mey dancing powerfully yet playfully, the effect was explosive. A new era in dance had begun. In the years to come De Keersmaeker was on the bill at the best theatres and festivals in the world and she snapped up all the most prestigious prizes.

Her stylistic characteristics of the early days were soon imitated: short graceful dresses, socks and lace-up boots, and also the brushing away of a lock of hair from the forehead, the straightening of a top that's slipping, and dancers who in a square formation move through the space in strong, rushing rhythms, falling, springing up, stepping, running, rolling, spiralling, in ambiguous moods of tight precision and relativising nonchalance; images that works like *Bartók, Aantekeningen* burnt into the retina.

The inspiration for her earliest works clearly originated in American postmodern minimalism. She was fascinated by mathematical structures such as the Fibonacci series. This sense of structure, monumental perfection and also of putting things into perspective can also be found in the many stage settings that Herman Sorgeloos has designed for *Rosas*. Sorgeloos has also captured De Keersmaeker's work in photos better than anyone else.

De Keersmaeker's dance nevertheless soon allowed for plenty of minor theatrical incidents, and many of the movements were carried out with relaxed nonchalance, so as to break down and relativise the rigidity of the geometric structures.

De Keersmaeker is a true dancer. She enjoys working in dance. But pure dance is unable to give her all the answers she is looking for. Little theatrical elements, such as an arch knowing glance, mischievous girlish coquetry or a forceful clenched fist to launch a movement have been increasingly creeping into her work as dramatic actions. They are expressions of jealousy, frustration, powerlessness, lunacy and love. And when words are better able to serve the message, the dancers use them, or else actors are brought in. Sometimes the sound is more significant than the content. In other productions the performers use words to scream out an emotion or to tell a story.

Heiner Müller's *Verkommenes Ufer, Medeamaterial, Landschaft mit Argonauten* (1987) was the first piece she directed as a play, and because of her great admiration for Bartók, she also tackled a Bluebeard opera. In *Just Before* (1997), *I said I* (1999) and *Quartett* (1999) the words were given even more impact. Conversely, in *Real Time* (1999), where the *Rosas* dancers performed together with actors from *Tg Stan*, she started from a blank sheet: no existing words, no existing score.

Throughout her artistic career, music, theatre, words and dance have in turn, and sometimes simultaneously, formed the thread of her compositional spirit. Whenever the opportunity arises, the musicians are invited to join the dancers on the stage so as to make the encounter between dance and music more direct and physical. In financial terms, this opportunity arose in 1992, when *Rosas*, the group

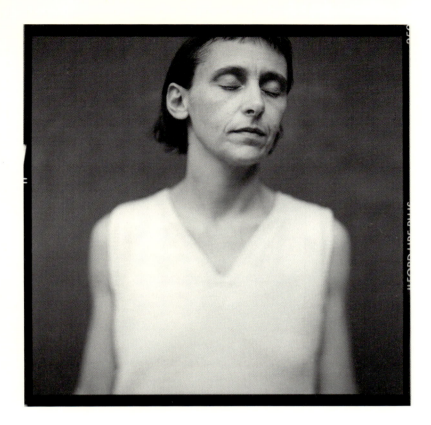

Photo S. Vanfleteren

De Keersmaeker established in 1983 and named after one of her works, became the 'company in residence' at the Brussels opera house, *De Munt*, at the invitation of its director Bernard Foccroulle. Then, after a short stay by the American choreographer Mark Morris, De Keersmaeker became Béjart's successor.

After the transparent minimalism of Steve Reich and Thierry de Mey, she sought greater complexity in the music of Bela Bartók, György Ligeti and Eugene Isaye. She subjected it to thorough analysis in order to construct effective responses in her dance structures. Later, composers from a more distant past also aroused her curiosity. In her dance, she formulated her own responses to the music of Bach, Monteverdi and Mozart: costume elements, even remnants of dance steps from the composers' era - simultaneously poisoned and charming - slip like an undertone into the austere contemporary dance.

In order to constantly challenge herself and her dance, she has entered into encounters with DJ Grazzhoppa and the musicians of the *Aka Moon* jazz group, who do not play according to tight fixed patterns and so elicit a different reaction from the dancers.

For the same reason one may in the course of a performance hear pop music hits, either to put things into perspective or as a counterweight to the 'serious' composi-

KINOK, 1994

Photo H. Sorgeloos

tions, or else Oriental music. De Keersmaeker once said that she did not even experience this as a clash of cultures: after all, we have heard music from past and present, from here and elsewhere, in our homes since we were children.

The way De Keersmaeker structures space, image, time and verbal content is evolving all the time. The movements initially corresponded to the compositions used. But more complex scores bring out different responses. Sometimes it is as if the dancers are hurried on by the music; at other times they work against it in counterpoint or deconstructively, as if the dancers' movements were intended to break down the musical structures and their own more obvious ones. Each confrontation offers an occasion to turn the art of dance in a new direction, and provide it with new sources of energy. This line is continued in *PARTS*, the school De Keersmaeker founded in 1995 and which already has an international reputation.

ANNE TERESA DE KEERSMAEKER
Mechelen, b. 1960

EDUCATION AND CAREER
Studied at *Mudra* in Brussels and the *Tisch School of the Arts* in New York.

In 1983 founded the *Rosas* company, which in 1992 became the 'company in residence' at the *Muntschouwburg* in Brussels. In 1995 founded the *PARTS* dance school in association with the *Muntschouwburg*.

WORKS
Fase, Four Movements to the Music of Steve Reich, 1982; *Rosas danst Rosas*, 1983; *Bartók, Aantekeningen*, 1986; *Mikrokosmos*, 1987; *Ottone, Ottone*, 1988; *Stella*, 1990; *Achterland*, 1990; *Erts*, 1992; *Mozart / Concert aria's. Un moto di gioia*, 1992; *Toccata*, 1993; *Kinok*, 1994; *Amor constante, más allá de la muerte*, 1994; *Erwartung / Verklärte Nacht*, 1995; *Woud, Three Movements of the Music of Berg, Schönberg and Wagner*, 1996; *Just Before*, 1997; *Duke Blue–Beard's Castle* (Mikrokosmos / Quattuor Nr. 4), 1998; *Drumming*, 1998; *I Said I*, 1999; *Quartett*, 1999; *Real Time*; 1999; *Rain*, 2001; *Small Hands*, 2001; *(But if a Look Should) April me*, 2002; *Once*, 2002

BIBLIOGRAPHY
Jef de Roeck, 'Anne Teresa de Keersmaeker ou la nouvelle danse en Flandre', in *Septentrion, revue de culture néerlandaise*, XV, 1986, no. 2, pp. 20-23.

Marianne van Kerkhoven, 'Tussen hemel en aarde. Een gesprek met Anne Teresa de Keersmaeker', in *Theaterschrift 2. The Written Space*, 1992, pp. 169-197; 'De besmetting tussen dans en muziek. Een gesprek met Anne Teresa de Keersmaeker en Thierry de Mey', in *Theaterschrift 9. Theatre and Music*, pp. 206-232.

Herman Sorgeloos, *Rosas album*, Theater Instituut Nederland, Amsterdam, 1993.

Deborah Jowitt, 'Adventuress in the Thickets of Postmodernism. A Reflection on the Work of Anne Teresa de Keersmaeker', in *The Low Countries. Arts and Society in Flanders and the Netherlands*, II, 1994-1995, pp. 59-62.

'Anne Teresa de Keersmaeker', *Portretten van podiumkunstenaars - Kritisch Theater Lexicon*, Vlaams Theater Instituut, Brussels, 1997 (also in English).

'Anne Teresa de Keersmaeker', in *Dietsche Warande en Belfort*, CXLVII, 2002, no. 2.

Rosas XX / Anne Teresa de Keersmaeker. Als en slechts als verwondering, La Renaissance du Livre, Tournai, 2002. *Rosas XX / Anne Teresa de Keersmaeker. If and Only If Wonder*, La Renaissance du Livre, Tournai, 2002. *Rosas XX / Anne Teresa de Keersmaeker. Si et seulement si étonnement*, La Renaissance du Livre, Tournai, 2002.

Pieter T'Jonck, 'Het werk is niet af, waarheid nooit uitgeschreven', in *Ons Erfdeel*, XLV, 2002, no. 5, pp. 685-693.

FILMS - VIDEOS - TELEVISION RECORDINGS
Hoppla!, Editions à voir, 1989; *Monologue by Fumiyo Ikeda at the End of Ottone / Ottone*, Editions à voir, 1990; *Ottone / Ottone I and II*, Editions à voir, 1991; *Rosa*, Editions à voir, 1992; *Mozart / Materiaal*, Editions à voir, 1993; *Achterland*, Editions à voir, 1994; *Tippeke*, Editions à voir, 1996; *Rosas danst Rosas*, Editions à voir, 1997; *Fase*, Editions à voir, 2002; *Rosas, vingt ans*, RTBF, 2002

ADDRESS
Rosas, Van Volxemlaan 164, B-1190 Brussel
Tel.: +32 (0)2 344 55 98   Fax: +32 (0)2 343 53 52
mail@rosas.be   www.rosas.be

Wim Vandekeybus

In 1987 Wim Vandekeybus danced a short duet with the painter Eduardo Torroja to Thierry de Mey's now renowned *Tafelpercussie* (Table Percussion). With tempestuous energy, strength and dexterity, they made daring leaps, launched themselves into the air in a backward curve, and smartly intercepted each other's falls... or not. They rolled over the floor, suddenly flung their bodies over with a thump, bounced up horizontally, over the other's body, all as if they were the playthings of an upward force. There was a chilling tension between the dancers and the audience.

Several months later the piece *What the Body Does Not Remember* opened at the *Toneelschuur* theatre in Haarlem (The Netherlands), the full-length expansion on the duet. 'Games' were played whose danger element put the audience on the edge of their seats. The dancers threw heavy stones at each other's heads, dropped razor-sharp darts into the boards between each other's feet, and threw themselves into the air to be caught at speed by a 'chance' passer-by. Every gesture had to stick to an absolutely precise timing, however rough and nonchalant it might have been. The dancers put their trust in and surrendered to the instinctive reactions to which the title refers, as tense as an animal in danger. The tone is set for the birth of a fascinating dance enterprise. Extreme tension, risk and conflict situations have remained constants in the work of Vandekeybus and his company *Ultima Vez* ('The Last Time').

The dancing in *What the Body...* is powered by an unflagging dynamic stirred up by the driving music of Thierry de Mey and Peter Vermeersch. In 1988 this work won a *Bessie Award* for 'a brutal confrontation of dance and music; the dangerous, combative landscape of 'What the Body does not remember'.'

Music is another stimulus for Vandekeybus, as in *The Weight of a Hand* (1990) and *Bereft of a Blissful Union* (1996), in which twelve musicians also occupied the stage. He has commissioned works from such standard-bearers of the music world as David Byrne (*In Spite of Wishing and Wanting*, 1999), Marc Ribot (*Inasmuch as Life is Borrowed*, 2000) and the DJ Yves de Mey, alias Eavesdropper (*Scratching the Inner Fields*, 2001).

But Vandekeybus, who was once a psychology student, also continues to be fascinated by the complex relationships between body and mind. He shows the vulnerability and strength of those who surrender to their reflexes or instincts in extreme circumstances, in conflicts, breaches and unpredictable, uncontrollable situations. It was with great tenderness and sympathy that he made the 89-year-old Carlo Verano, a former variety artist, the subject of several of his pieces, and brought a blind dancer into his company, who before our very eyes evolved from a fearful little creature feeling his way forward and guided by the other dancers, to a self-assured independent dancer and a captivating stage personality (Said Gharbi created the first performance of his own in 2002!).

Film and video are Vandekeybus' other fascinations (he once studied photography too). The images jumble up the order the dance brings to the space, amplify its energy and give it a totally new dynamic and literally a new dimension in a new rhythm and its own visual design. But they also introduce other places and moments in time into the here and now of the performance. He has also won several prizes for his short films.

Photo S. Vanfleteren

Vandekeybus was once an actor in Jan Fabre's *De macht der theaterlijke dwaas-heden*. He increasingly introduces theatrical and anecdotal elements into his work, which lead to extreme, fascinating and often even poetic moments. More intimacy and even tenderness is gradually nestling between the violent, hyper-dynamic and rough scenes in which partners passionately or aggressively draw in then repulse each other, and this takes the form of fond touches and embraces, among other things. The driving current of energy that alternately pushes the dance forward and knocks it off course in fitful counterthrusts now quietens down more often, like an abated storm.

Words have crept in in a charming way, such as in the marvellous short film called *The Last Words*, based on two surrealist short stories by Julio Cortázar and screened during *In Spite of Wishing and Wanting*. He collaborated with the Flemish writer Peter Verhelst for the text of *Scratching the Inner Fields*. Verhelst also kept track of work on *Blush* (2002), a piece about isolation and liberation, for which he adapted and arranged the spoken material contributed by the performers. Around this, Vandekeybus arranged an inexhaustible play of dancers who, like powerful, streaking, spinning fireballs, skim past each other, dragging a third with them on the way, and then spiral apart looking for a new tack, till ultimately all that is left is

HER BODY DOESN'T FIT
HER SOUL, 1993

Photo D. Willems

a shimmer of steam. In *Metamorphoses* (2003) Vandekeybus will even be tackling Ovid, together with actors from the Dutch theatre company *Toneelgroep Amsterdam* and dancers from *Ultima Vez*.

This piece will focus on actor-dancers on the stage or in the projected films, close at hand or far away, in another country or another stage set. These people are presented because of their personality and each brings their own world with them, with their feelings, thoughts and acting, still virginally unshaped by the theatre, like the old eccentric Carlo Verano in *Immer das Selbe gelogen* and the blind dancers in *Her Body Doesn't Fit Her Soul*.

Dance, music and film appear to want to manipulate time, slow it down, speed it up, even go beyond it. The boundaries between sense and nonsense, beautiful and ugly, the imaginary and the concrete, between theatre and reality, are no longer under discussion. Vandekeybus continues to push art itself over the boundaries.

WIM VANDEKEYBUS
Herenthout, b. 1963

EDUCATION AND CAREER
Originally studied psychology and photography.
Took courses in classical dance, modern dance and tango.

Travelled the world for two years in Jan Fabre's piece *De macht der theaterlijke dwaasheden*.
Since 1987 has created choreographic work for his own company, *Ultima Vez*.

WORKS
What the Body Does Not Remember, 1987; *Les porteuses de mauvaises nouvelles*, 1989; *The Weight of a Hand*, 1990; *Immer das Selbe gelogen*, 1991; *Her Body Doesn't Fit Her Soul*, 1993; *Mountains Made of Barking*, 1994; *Alle Grössen decken sich zu*, 1995; *Bereft of a Blissful Union*, 1996; *7 for a Secret Never to Be Told*, 1997; *In Spite of Wishing and Wanting*, 1999; *Inasmuch as Life Is Borrowed*, 2000; *Scratching the Inner Fields*, 2001, *Blush*, 2002

BIBLIOGRAPHY
Kisselgoff, Anna, 'A New Work by Wim Vandekeybus', in *The New York Times*, 22 November 1987.
Kisselgoff, Anna, 'Maximum-Energy Minimalism', in *The New York Times*, 28 October 1989.
Carmen del Val, 'Despliegue escénico', in *El País*, 19 January 1990.
Mountains Made of Barking: Wim Vandekeybus, Ultima Vez, Kritak, Leuven, 1994 (articles in Dutch, French and English).
Sigrid Bousset, 'Lichamen in vrije val', in *Etcetera*, XIII, 1995, no. 9, pp. 13-16.
Yvonne Beljaars, 'Wim Vandekeybus en Ultima Vez: een vat met teveel inhoud', in *Dans*, XIV, 1996, no. 5.
Dominique Frétard, 'Le chorégraphe Wim Vandekeybus et ses paniques postpsychédéliques éclatent les limites du réel', in *Le Monde*, 23 March 1996.
Carmen del Val, 'Plumas como dardos', in *El País*, 25 July 1997.
'Wim Vandekeybus', *Portretten van podiumkunstenaars – Kritisch Theater Lexicon*, Vlaams Theater Instituut, Brussels, 1997 (also in English).
Rosita Boisseau, 'Douze hommes en proie à une peur animale', in *Le Monde*, 6 July 1999.
Giuseppe Videtti, 'Un sogno che si chiama desiderio', in *La Repubblica*, 15 March 1999.

FILMS - VIDEOS - TELEVISION RECORDINGS
Roseland, Beeldhuis, 1990; *La Mentira*, Addison de Wit, 1992; *Elba and Federico*, Carlo Verano, 1993; Saïd and Mary, Anne Quirynen, 1994, *Bereft of a Blissful Union*, De Filmfabriek / Anne Quirynen, 1996; *Silver*, Quasi Modo, 1997; *In Spite of Wishing and Wanting*, Quasi Modo, 1999; *The Last Words*, Itinera Films, 1999; *Inasmuch as Life Is Borrowed*, Quasi Modo, 2000

ADDRESS
Ultima Vez, Koolmijnenkaai 34, B-1080 Brussel
Tel.: +32 (0)2 219 55 28
Fax: +32 (0)2 219 68 02
info@ultimavez.com
www.ultimavez.com

Alain Platel made his debut in 1984 with *Stabat Mater*, which he created with friends (the video film-maker Johan Grimonprez) and family (his sister, the play-maker Pascale Platel) in his own living room. For the first ten years, he and his company *Les Ballets C(omtemporains) de la B(elgique)*, surrealistically named in the Magritte style, remained in the shadow of the other Flemish dance groups of the eighties, while working on his own absurd form of dance theatre, for which the critics thought up an endless series of points of reference and labels. In *Emma* (1988), for example, the female protagonist directed a Fellini-like circus troupe of dancers and musicians who, in a visual slapstick style, earnestly and deliberately carried out the most idiotic movements and continually produced unnecessary props from a huge travelling trunk.

From 1993 an increase in scale took place in Platel's work and he also engaged international professional dancers for the first time, who, alongside his own 'family' of self-taught performers and children (who were more than a stylistic feature, and in fact symbolised the vulnerability of his world), performed in large-scale orchestrated productions. In order to fulfil his production aims he and *Les Ballets C de la B* became the resident company at *Kunstencentrum Vooruit* (Vooruit Arts Centre) in Ghent. In collaboration with the playwright Arne Sierens and the *Victoria* production company, a second, more text-oriented approach developed parallel to the dance theatre. In this way he built up a masterly body of work which in 2001 was awarded the prestigious 'European Prize for New Theatre Realities'.

Alain Platel believes in the baroque theory that music has the power to heal. In his pieces, therefore, live classical music is both a counterpoint to and a safety valve for the intense emotions expressed in the movement. In his dance theatre trilogy, comprising *Bonjour Madame, ...* (1993), *La Tristeza Complice* (1995) and *Iets op Bach* (Something set to Bach, 1997) Platel had his favourite baroque music played live: this included Purcell, which Dick van der Harst arranged for an orchestra of accordion-players in *La Tristeza Complice*, and Bach cantatas played by a chamber ensemble led by the cellist Roel Dieltiens in *Iets op Bach*. This heavenly music contrasted with the worldly, sometimes unpleasant but always profoundly human and loving look at the seamy side of society.

Platel always creates his pieces in Ghent. His stage settings vary from stylised depictions to literal copies of a square in Ghent, workman's houses and interiors. Together with the playwright Arne Sierens, Platel opts for the 'ordinariness and reality' of disjointed working-class families (in *Moeder en Kind* - Mother and Child) and *Allemaal Indiaan* (We're all Indians Now)) or a troupe of fairground or circus people (in *Bernadetje* and *Iets op Bach*). This choice is primarily a formal, aesthetic statement whereby Platel and Sierens subscribe to Tadeusz Kantor's adage that 'in art one only penetrates to the universal by depicting the most concrete and banal'.

Rather than developing his own idiom of movement, Platel always leaves plenty of room for his dancers' personalities and prefers to play off against each other the eclectic diversity and contrasts between them. In addition, as a remedial educationalist he is interested mainly in 'deviant behaviour', inspired both motorically and verbally by particular pathological conditions such as Tourette's syndrome (in *La Tristeza Complice*).

Photo S. Vanfleteren

As a result of Platel's stimulation of his dancers' own development, several of them have emerged from under his wing and generated their own artistic work. *Les Ballets C de la B* was then quickly organised as a collective to produce the work of Koen Augustijnen, Christine de Smedt, Sidi Larbi Cherkaoui and Hans van den Broeck in addition to that of Platel himself.

Hans van den Broeck was the first to follow in his teacher's footsteps. He incorporates his knowledge of and penchant for film into the structure, formal vocabulary (such as deliberate deceleration), content and images, all with the same surrealist and absurd approach. In the stage setting for *Everyman* (1994), for example, home videos supplement the story of a dysfunctional family portrayed in movement.

Christine de Smedt's choreographic work is limited to a solo and a group piece for 81 dancers, with 9 professional dancers supervising 72 non-professionals in a playfully structured, partly improvised choreography that fires critical shots at the consumer society.

Koen Augustijnen is probably the most eclectic member of the collective. He does the choreography for plays directed by Ivo van Hove, works with a stilt-theatre group in Australia, performs with the Antwerp rock bands dEUS and Zita Swoon and

Iets op Bach (Something
set to Bach)**, 1997**

Photo Chr. van der Burght   has created a solo for the French-Chilean hiphop dancer Ernesto Cortez. In his work
for *Les Ballets C de la B* he combines his love of the most varied forms of music (from
Bach on electric guitar to an actual rock concert with *Zita Swoon*, in *Plage Tattoo*)
with a humorous exploration of the contrasts between man and woman.

The Moroccan Belgian Sidi Larbi Cherkaoui is the youngest and also the most
promising offspring of the Platel family. After a broad-based dance education in
which he combined classical training (*Hoger Instituut voor Dans* in Lier-Antwerp)
with a year at *PARTS*, Anne Teresa de Keersmaeker's contemporary dance course,
and show and jazz dance on popular television programmes, in 1997 he ended up
at *Les Ballets*, where he was a brilliant soloist in *Iets op Bach*. In his own *Rien de Rien*
he converted all his influences and knowledge into a richly nuanced political
statement on the tensions that arise when dance styles, cultures and religions are
brought face to face.

ALAIN PLATEL
Ghent, b. 1956

EDUCATION AND CAREER
Remedial educationalist. Studied mime (under Marcel Hoste and others) and contemporary dance (under Barbara Pearce and others).

In 1984 founded his own company, *Les Ballets C(ontemporains) de la B(elgique)*.

Other choreographers in the collective: Koen Augustijnen, Hans van den Broeck (till the end of december 2002), Sidi Larbi Cherkaoui, Christine de Smedt.

WORKS
Stabat Mater, 1984; *Lichte Kavalerie*, 1985; *Mange P'tit Coucou*, 1986 ; *Emma*, 1988; *O Boom*, 1989; *Mussen*, 1991; *Bonjour Madame, comment allez-vous aujourd'hui il fait beau, il va sans doute pleuvoir, etcetera*, 1993; *Moeder en Kind*, 1994; *La Tristeza Complice*, 1995; *Bernadetje*, 1996; *Iets op Bach*, 1997; *Allemaal Indiaan*, 1999

BIBLIOGRAPHY
Jan Baart, 'Les Ballets C de la B', in *Dans*, XIV, 1996, no. 6.
'Alain Platel', in *Etcetera*, XV, 1997, no. 60, pp. 61-62.
Peter van Bouwel, 'De Bach-verslaving van Alain Platel', in *Theatermaker*, III, 1999, no. 6, pp. 22-27.
Gie Goris, 'Alice Walker en Alain Platel: goedheid en kwetsbaarheid zijn ongewoon', in *Wereldwijd*, 1999, no. 298, pp. 32-35.
Steven de Belder, 'Hard schreeuwen om het gevaar af te houden: het theaterwerk van Alain Platel', in *Ons Erfdeel*, XLIV, 2001, no. 2, pp. 249-255.
Alain Platel, Dis Voir, Paris, 2002.

ADDRESS
Les Ballets C de la B, Citadellaan 40, B-9000 Gent
Tel.: +32 (0)9 221 75 01
Fax: +32 (0)9 221 81 72
info@lesballetscdela.be

Marc Vanrunxt

When Jan Fabre made *Het is theater zoals te verwachten en te voorzien was* in 1982, he asked a choreographer for advice on movement. This was Marc Vanrunxt, who had just completed his dance training under An Slootmaekers, who was loyal to Laban's school of East European expressionism as well as that of Rosalia Chladeck. After one piece for Slootmaekers' company, Vanrunxt presented his first fully independent choreography in an empty house in 1981. It was the middle of winter, the audience was wrapped in blankets, and a young woman danced in water and with her wet hair flung drops of water in every direction. The performance area for the following item was the narrow strip provided by the mantelpiece, and then the garden was the setting for a solo. In these pieces, Vanrunxt continued to dance in vague terms, with words and reason meaning nothing, but where other powers and forces carry you along in what the Japanese call *Ma*, somewhere between understanding and feeling, between life and death.

From 1982 to 1984 he created four short dances, furious movements driven by energies whose source is some deep emotion. However, these sources have no need of a story. In *Solo voor duizend mannen* (Solo for a Thousand Men) Vanrunxt has to compete with the raging force of Penderecki's *Threnos*. Two men run up and down in overlong wide skirts that flap behind them pathetically. In *No puedo más* (I Cannot Go On) Vanrunxt, wrapped in bandages from head to toe, fights against his restricted freedom of movement. Whenever he falls during his furious struggle, he has to be stood up again. He resumes the struggle again and again, until his fury subsides, when the bandages gradually slip from their positions and liberation does not bring joy, but a 'cruel' calm. The fight against restrictions recurs in *Poging tot beweging* (Attempt to Move), his first choreography for a group of dancers. This time they are sitting wrapped in paper. They pry and burrow their way out and then comes the liberating dance. After this liberation, the space is gradually occupied and 'time' takes on another meaning. The same thing happens in his subsequent pieces. He works very precisely, with every stage of the evolution of his dance drawn on paper. The dances that come about in this way are more restful and serene.

The raging, often masochistic violence is replaced by a deliberate use of time and space. Structures arise, but still on the basis of various questions: what happens and when? When I compose beautiful images, when I break structures down, when I bring beauty and ugliness and kitsch face to face? Sometimes Vanrunxt puts all the elements one after the other, clearly separated, like a consummate minimalist, and at other times his work is more vague, with a single signal given several meanings. In this way, simplicity and slowness can yet, in their various layers, radiate a powerful tension. In such pieces as *Hyena* (1985), which is also the name of his organisation, *Ballet in wit* (Ballet in White, 1988) and *Moderne compositie* (1990) the agitation gives way to restfulness and beauty without anxiety. This is sustained by the simplicity of puritanism, reduction, monochromy and minimalism, promptly compensated for by magical-kitsch insertions, pathetic exaggerations, pleonasm, excess, ambiguity and witty asides. A performance may lapse from a solemn ritual or ceremony into exuberant desacralising outbursts. As in *A.dieu* (1986) in which the dancers, after a solemn purification ritual, wrapped in black silk crinolines with bustle, break out into a barbaric *French Cancan* set to

Photo S. Vanfleteren

vaguely recognisable music by Offenbach, with delicate yet sensual movements, impetuous leaps and hallucinatory centrifugal spiral movements.

Skirts have continued to appear in Vanrunxt's work ever since those overlong ones in *Solo voor duizend mannen*. They are usually long and wide, and sometimes painted with symbols. Vanrunxt initially designed the costumes himself, together with his dancer and associate Eric Raeves, who since then has also made a name for himself as a captivating choreographer. For more recent pieces he has drawn on the collections of such Belgian designers as Martin Margiella and Ann de Meulemeester. Vanrunxt likes to involve other artists. Anne-Mie van Kerckhoven makes sets and video films. Robert Cash paints dresses. Other figures from the history of art and dance provide him with inspiration: Oskar Schlemmer, Gerhard Bohner, Loïe Fuller, Elsworth Kelly, Barnett Newman and many more.

Thierry Génicot has supplied several musical montages. The main role of music in Vanrunxt's work is to set the atmosphere. Here too he likes extremes. Alongside pieces by Pachelbel, Hindemith, Penderecki, Gorecki and Ustvolskaya and new compositions by Karel Goeyvaerts, Thierry Génicot, Harry de Wit and Serge Verstockt, and also pop music by Yoko Ono, the Virgin Prunes, Siouxsie and the Banshees and Lou Reed, he uses with equal seriousness and respect schmaltzy

KULT-STAR, 1993

Photo M.-L. Dooyes

popular songs by Petula Clark, Brigitte Bardot and Dalida.

In the 1990s, the strict pattern in which Vanrunxt had always structured space and time became too restricting for him. He now allowed the dancers to take their own course, within or crossing the boundaries of structures and patterns, confident that the energy of the dancers and the space would evolve into exciting synergies, which would then enter into a symbiosis with the audience: a process of organic growth that no longer arose on the drawing board but in the studio (or even more daringly, on stage). *Fortitudo* (1997), *Antropomorf* (1998) and *Antimaterie* (1999) are free of symbols and messages. The medium itself is the message. It is closer to the experience of the audience and is more fragile. Vanrunxt continues to ask questions and look for answers (*Some Problems of Space Perception*, 2001)

Throughout his career, Vanrunxt has continued to dance in pieces by such colleagues as Pauline Daniëls, Thierry Smits, Truus Bronkhorst and especially Jan Fabre, who created the extravagant solo *The Pickwick Man* for him.

MARC VANRUNXT
Antwerp, b. 1960

EDUCATION AND CAREER
Self-taught.

From 1976 to 1981 danced in An Slootmaekers' *Dansschool* and *Dansgroep*.
From 1978 to 1981 took a variety of dance courses and workshops at home and abroad.
Presented his own work from 1981.
In 1984 founded his own work organisation called *Hyena*, which was later incorporated into *Kunst / Werk*.
In 2001 was the temporary artistic director of the *De Beweeging* festival.
Is a guest teacher on the mime course at the *Amsterdamse Theaterschool* and at the *Hoger Instituut voor Dans* in Lier - Antwerp.

WORKS
Dans over steden, gebouwen en kleuren, 1981; *Lente '82*, 1982; *Solo voor duizend mannen*, 1982; *No puedo más*, 1983; *Absolute Körperkontrolle*, 1984; *Poging tot beweging*, 1984; *Hyena*, 1985; *Aï*, 1986; *A.dieu*, 1986; *Ballet battage*, 1987; *Ballet in wit*, 1988; *Sst, de natuur is dood*, 1989; *Moderne compositie*, 1990; *Sur scène*, 1991; *Triomf of dood*, 1992; *Kult-Star*, 1993; *The Power of Love*, 1994; *Dies Irae*, 1995; *Ex-Voto*, 1996; *Fortitudo*, 1997; *Mijn solo voor Marie (vernietigd)*, 1998; *Antropomorf*, 1998; *Private Collection*, 1999; *Antimaterie*, 1999; *Performer*, 2000; *Some Problems of Space Perception*, 2001; *Most Recent*, 2002

BIBLIOGRAPHY
Katie Verstockt, 'Is dit nog ballet, is het al theater of iets helemaal nieuws', in *Etcetera*, I, 1983, pp. 46-48.
Katie Verstockt, 'Marc Vanrunxt kijkt om' in *Etcetera*, IV, 1986, no. 24.
Katie Verstockt, 'Beauté visuelle du Kitsch', in *Art et Culture*, 8 April 1991.
Thierry Génicot, 'Marc Vanrunxt, un parcours singulier', in *Nouvelles de danse*, XI, May 1992, pp. 24-29.
Myriam van Imschoot, 'Een salon van weigeraars', in *Etcetera*, XIV, December 1996, pp. 36-39.
Myriam van Imschoot, 'Comètes et planètes. Marc Vanrunxt, danseur et chorégraphe', in *Carnet*, 1997, no. 13, pp. 24-29 (also in English).
'Marc Vanrunxt', in *Portretten van podiumkunstenaars - Kritisch Theater Lexicon*, Vlaams Theater Instituut, Brussels, 1997 (also in English).
Pascal Gielen, 'Marc Vanrunxt en de restauratie van het rituele lichaam', in *Etcetera*, XVII, 1999, no. 67, pp. 55-58.
Rob de Graaf, 'Marc Vanrunxt: tussen de aarde en de oneindigheid', in *TM*, V, no. 8, 2001, pp. 44-46.

FILMS - VIDEOS - TELEVISION RECORDINGS
De vier uitersten, Zeno X Gallery, 1984; *Bewegend gezelschap maakt gebaren (zonder melodrama)*, Theaterschool Amsterdam, 1986; *Victoria*, VTI, 1989; *Ballet in Wit*, BRT, 1990; *Avenue de l'Hippodrome*, RTBF, 1991; *Fragment of the Seven Veils*, Argos, 1991; *Persona*, De Beweeging, 1997; Ogni pensiero vola, De Andere Film, 1997

ADDRESS
Van den Nestlei 11 A, B-2018 Antwerpen
Tel.: +32 (0)3 233 32 36
cderycke@kunst.werk.be

Karin Vyncke

During the third edition of the *De Beweeging* festival (1987), Karin Vyncke presented *Sous les vêtements blancs*. A woman on the edge of insanity. The area looks like a deserted chicken run: a worn-out sofa, a rickety ladder, a carpet of white feathers which whirl up as a result of the dancers' boisterous performance. The audience watches from behind chicken wire. Vyncke speaks a no-nonsense, visceral dance language, which gives raw and uncivilized expression to what goes on in the mind, without worrying about the aesthetics, but creating powerful images which cling to the retina. Her partner, Yoris van den Houte, creates the forceful sets which, just like the dancing, situate her approach in the same atmosphere as that of *Arte Povera* and *Poor Theatre*. Grotowski, Kantor and Artaud (*Théâtre de la cruauté*) are never far off. The avenues of thought also lead to dance theatre – not that of Pina Bausch but rather the innovative style of Maguy Marin and Josef Nadj and the Japanese *butoh*, which also examines the margins of life and explores the field of intuition between body and mind, between reason and sentiment. It is no coincidence that several of Vyncke's dancers have experience with *butoh* and in 2001 she went to Japan herself to participate in a workshop with Min Tanaka.

Vyncke followed a classical training, studied under Grotowski, spent a few months in New York to take lessons in contemporary dance, studied in Paris under Peter Goss and danced in Germany under the guidance of Gerhard Bohner and Reinhild Hoffman. But her most valuable training was the six years she spent with Maguy Marin. She created her first choreography for Marin's company: *Glue*. In 2002, one of Vyncke's works premiered in a co-production with the *Cie Maguy Marin*.

After creating a piece for the *Centre national de danse contemporaine* in Angers she continued to work in France for a while. It was here that *Sous les vêtements blancs* came into being. At the *Concours international de chorégraphie* in Bagnolet she was awarded a video production with *C.A.C.-Montbéliard* and a residency in *La Ménagerie de verre* in Paris. The video production was an example of image and rhythm manipulation, which heralded a new era of video dance and in its turn carried off prizes at the Dance Video Festival in Sète.

Internal confusion, dualism, existential doubts, fear, longing and loneliness, aggression and rejection are present throughout Vyncke's work. Often in extremes: panic, obsession, passion, but also power, impotence, abuse of power and manipulation are recurring themes. The characters fit awkwardly within the group, through insubordination or inappropriate behaviour. In *Kreuset* (1990), the dancers, crazed by thirst, are driven to compulsively violent dancing. The energy hangs in visible streaks in the air, ricocheting off the zinc wall of the set until it causes pain in the mind of the audience. In *Mé-zon* (1989) we see man searching for a home, for family affection. In *Vous avez appris que je tombais* (1992), confused people roam, torn in a struggle between chaotic, passionate desire, and sober, clear reasoning. The tragicomic buffoon in *Could Can Be* (1995) knows how, with refinement, to turn the tables on leaders and simpletons, victims and fools. In *Tar*, Vyncke responds to the work by the untimely deceased American graffiti artist Jean-Michel Basquiat, with imperceptible, tangled amalgams and confusions of images, movements and people: a dance just as chaotic as the uprooting effect of city life. *Tar* is concerned with loneliness, power and alienation, the desperate instinct for survival. Androgy-

Photo S. Vanfleteren

nous women and confused introvert men, searching for alliance, repel each other, clumsily disrupt the peace and develop aggression whilst intending to be gentle. Cynical-sadistic manipulations and convulsive pulling and twisting movements result in forceful, resolutely articulate dance sequences. Tension, trembling and spasm become an obsessional dance which is able to evolve into conciliatory, neatly choreographed dance.

In *And Yet Not without Wandering about* (2000), an artist once again provides the inspiration: the Jewish-Iranian Choreh Feyzdjou. Yoris van de Houte once more brings to the stage a number of endearingly simple objects, which redefine the look of the set. Rolls of fabric painted black stand upright for a change, filling the area with phallic columns, then they are positioned horizontally, or perhaps float in space, resting on two small upturned garden tables; dark, horizontal stripes which inject architectural structure into the dull white space. The dancers enter nonchalantly into partnerships with the horizontality and verticality of the objects, gyrating in the churned up dust. Material often has a part to play in Vyncke's scheme of things: the feathers in *Sous les vêtements blancs*, running water in *Kreuset*, paint in *Palimpsest* (1998), where she steps into a paint tray and then calmly dances out figures on a blank sheet of paper.

BEAUTY FREE, 1996
Photo M. Hoflack /
SOFAM - Belgium

The conspicuous (or inconspicuous) break-dance movements which have crept in (especially those by Julien Faure) are not exploited to the extreme. They are rather the organic carrier of driving forces which we do not know but by which, to the accompaniment of Nicolas Roseeuw's music, we are drawn along. They are evidence of a bizarre convergence of images, objects, movements, people and sounds.

The states of the soul are abstracted into a ritual, a surprising, fascinating spectacle, a poetic interplay of the cruel and the unpleasant. The material essence of the body acquires the dimension of a close-up and becomes a reference point, as it is less changeable than the internal psyche. This is Karin Vyncke at her best.

KARIN VYNCKE
Brussels, b. 1960

EDUCATION AND CAREER
Classical training under Marina van Hoeck.
Trained in contemporary dance in New York and Paris.
Danced with Gerhard Bohner and Reinhild Hoffman.

Did her first choreographic pieces in the studios of Maguy Marin (Paris).
Originally worked with her own company, *Compagnie Karin Vyncke* in France, but settled in Belgium in 1992.

WORKS
Glue (1985); *Next* (1986); *Sous les vêtements blancs*, 1987; *Mé-zon*, 1989; *Kreuset*, 1990; *Vous avez appris que je tombais*, 1992; *All Shall Be Well*, 1992 en 1994 ; *Winternacht*, 1993; *Could Can Be*, 1995; *Nerf, febr. '9**, 1996; *Beauty Free*, 1996; *Vlasnaald*, 1997; *Tar*, 1998; *Upside down*, 1998; *Palimpsest*, 1998; *Sugar / Baby / Love*, 1999; *And Yet Not without Wandering about*, 2000; *Shotdance*, 2000; *La comptesse bourgeoise*, 2001; *Vlug Stuk*, 2002

BIBLIOGRAPHY
Claire Diez, 'Karin Vyncke, danses et cadenses', in *La Libre Culture*, no. 79, 8 May 1991, p. 4 (interview).
Katie Verstockt, 'And Yet Not without Wandering about', in *De Scène*, XIIL, 2000, no. 396, p. 14.

FILMS - VIDEOS - TELEVISION RECORDINGS
Sous les vêtements blancs, Patrick Zanoli, 1989; *Tristitia*, BRTN, 1992; *Lena's verhaal*, Aquilon / Vooruit, 1995

ADDRESS
Compagnie Karin Vyncke, Fortstraat 35, B-1060 Sint-Gillis
Tel.: +32 (0)2 541 01 73
Fax: +32 (0)2 541 01 77
karin.vyncke@pi.be

Meg Stuart

The American Meg Stuart made her debut with *Disfigure Study*, a full-length show, during the 1991 *Klapstukfestival* and since then has been developing her international career using Leuven and Brussels as a home base where, in 1994, she formed *Damaged Goods*, not a company but a production organisation.

Both the title of her debut and her organisation are exemplary of what the international reviews term 'victim art'. Stuart shows the body in its nakedness and in its ugliness. This choice of the 'disfigured' and 'damaged' body is at times an explicit, political choice as in the solo *XXX for Arlene and Colleagues* (1995), made in reaction to the puritanical American dance critics who disapproved of the Aids theme as a subject for a dance performance. But in addition it is primarily a formal choice, a research method which emanates from Stuart's fascination with the visual arts.

Stuart's choreographic oeuvre has been developed in collaboration with trend-setting visual artists. The term 'study' in the title of her debut is just as significant as the adjective 'disfigured'. Her choice of fragmenting the body, zooming in on details and the continual experimentation with the audience's view show similarities with anatomical studies in painting. The 'twisting' and 'coiling' are lively three-dimensional interpretations of the pluralistic perspective acquired from Cubism.

The set design by the American painter Lawrence Carrol for the performance *No One is Watching* (1995) resembles a painter's studio. Whereas in the first two productions the individual body was analysed like a sculpture, in this 'studio' six bodies explore each other in changing combinations: for example, without touching each other, in a sensual circular dance, or falling on each other's neck with increasing violence and like a writhing heap of limbs thrown on top of each other.

With her *Insert Skin* project, Stuart entered more explicitly into a dialogue with the visual. In four episodes, she engages in dialogue with four visual artists: the Fleming Lawrence Malstaf, the Canadian designer Bruce Mau and the American artists Gary Hill and Anne Hamilton. In *Splayed Mind Out* (1997), created in collaboration with video artist Gary Hill, Stuart used the techniques and insights of the video artist to take her research into the audience perspective a step further.

The American Anne Hamilton is primarily known for her installations and performances, in which she uses natural materials to stimulate the senses of the audience. For *Appetite* (1998), Stuart's most playful and accessible choreography, she designed a set in which everything is covered in a layer of clay which dries out during the performance. In the first part the dancers leave their footprints and traces of other parts of their body in the wet clay, and these evaporate and disappear into dust as the performance progresses.

The transience of time, the central 'here and now' theme of the performance is another important element in Stuart's work. Parallel with the *Insert Skin* series she created a number of large-scale improvisation projects: *Crash Landing @ Leuven*, *Vienna*, *Paris*, *Lisbon* and *Moscow*, in which she challenged changing combinations of dancers, musicians and visual artists to dialogue with each other and the location through imposed 'tasks' and research assignments. With these improvisation projects she registered her name in the history of dance as the heiress to the New

Photo S. Vanfleteren

York Judson Group and in her turn influenced a new generation of choreographers including Christine de Smedt and David Hernandez.

Since 2001, *Damaged Goods'* operations have been recognized and subsidised by the Ministry of the Flemish Community. Furthermore, Stuart was offered a residency at Christopher Marthaler's *Zürich Schauspielhaus*, so that she could expand her fundamental movement research to embrace theatre and language. Recently she has been offered a residency at the *Volksbühne Rosa-Luxemburg-Platz* in Berlin. As the standard-bearer of a new generation of dance artists who have been emancipating dance since the nineties, Stuart summarises the movement in five points: '1. The movement from autonomous dance to the autonomous body; 2. The movement from composition to improvisation; 3. The movement from stage design to performing visual art in the theatre; 4. The movement from dance companies to project collaboration; 5. The movement from performance to intervention.'

For the moment her work has reached its peak in a new series of happenings called *Highway 101*, started in 2001 in diverse locations, from the intimate surroundings of the *Kaaitheater* studios in Brussels, through large industrial spaces in Rotterdam and Vienna, to the public space of the central entrance hall of the Pompidou Centre in Paris. For each version of *Highway 101*, Stuart designs a circuit,

APPETITE, 1998
Photo Chr. van der Burght

drawing on a repertory of mini-choreographic pieces – for example, the masterly dance duets between a dancer and the body of his partner as projected on to a sand table – which she rethinks according to the location and to which she adds unique, often improvised sequences. Once again, the experimentation with the audience perspective is pivotal: inside and out, above and below; whether live or virtual, the interplay continues in an ambiguous and often whimsical manner.

In *ALIBI* (2001) Stuart returns to a classical theatre arrangement. She explores a number of the achievements of spoken theatre with her new artistic partners (including the monumental set designed by Anna Viebrock and text excerpts written by the British stage director Tim Etchells) to which she adds her own deconstructive style characteristics, resulting in a flood of images alluding to our contemporary condition.

MEG STUART

New Orleans (United States), b. 1965

EDUCATION AND CAREER

Bachelor of Fine Arts Degree in Dance at *New York State University*.
Dancer and assistant choreographer with the *Randy Warshaw Dance Company*.

In 1994 founded her own company, *Damaged Goods*.

WORKS

Disfigure Study, 1991; *No Longer Readymade*, 1993; *Swallow my Yellow Smile* (created with Via Lewandowsky), 1994; *No One Is Watching*, 1995; *XXX for Arlene and Colleagues*, 1995; *Crash Landing*, 1996-1999; *Insert Skin 1 – They Live in Our Breath* (created with Lawrence Malstaf), 1996; *Remote* (created with Bruce Mau for Mikhail Baryshnikov's *White Oak Dance Project*), 1997; *Splayed Mind Out* (created with Gary Hill), 1997; *Appetite* (created with Ann Hamilton), 1998; *A Choreographic Laboratory*, 1999; *Highway 101* (created with, among others, Jorge León and Stefan Pucher), 2000-2001; *ALIBI*, 2001

BIBLIOGRAPHY

Rudi Laermans & Pieter T'Jonck, *Esbracejar, Physical Paradoxes*: Vera Mantero, Meg Stuart, Klapstuk, Leuven, 1993.

Johan Reyniers, 'Tien Cunninghams cadeau voor één Meg Stuart en één Bill T. Jones', in *Etcetera*, XI, 1993, no. 40, pp. 26-28.

Patrick de Spiegelaere, 'Meg Stuart: No One Is Watching', in *Dietsche Warande en Belfort*, CXL, 1995, no. 5, pp. 561-571.

Rudi Laermans, 'De denkbeeldige lichamen van Meg Stuart', in *Etcetera*, XV, 1997, no. 60, pp. 29-33.

Rudi Laermans, Jeroen Peeters, Jan Ritsema & Tine van Aerschot, 'Meg Stuart', in *A-Prior*, no. 6, 2001-2002.

ADDRESS

Damaged Goods, Onze-Lieve-Vrouw Van Vaakstraat 83, B-1000 Brussel
Tel.: +32 (0)2 513 25 40
Fax: +32 (0)2 513 22 48
damaged.goods@village.uunet.be
www.damagedgoods.be

Abdelaziz Sarrokh

In the nineties 'diversity' was very much the buzzword of the dance world. Styles, genres and media were mixed: contemporary and classical dancers, non-dancers, actors and musicians stood side by side on stage. Choreographers introduced streetwise young virtuosi of the hip-hop culture. Scrambled steps, dives and other break-dance 'moves' made their appearance, polished up and put to use. But there was still no hint of collaboration, as had been the case in the United States and France. Alain Platel provided a significant impetus by inviting young break-dancers to participate in *De Beste Belgische Danssolo*, and a little later having the break-dancer Abdelaziz Sarrokh dance in his shows (*Bonjour Madame* ... and *La Tristeza Complice*).

When, in 1996, the Berchem Cultural Centre (close to Antwerp) wanted to undertake a socio-cultural project with young dancers of every persuasion, it was clear that Abdelaziz Sarrokh was the obvious person to steer this project successfully. Sarrokh was born in Morocco and immigrated to Belgium as a child. After training as an electrician he became a social worker dealing with the homeless of the city of Ghent. He is no stranger to cultural diversity. Meanwhile he has emerged as a gifted dancer (and break-dancer); he even has his own dance group (*Al Fath*) and has collaborated on several theatre pieces.

In Berchem he was faced with a female African dancer, trained in both classical and contemporary dance, an unyielding self-taught dancer and top-level break-dancers who plunge into the arena to perform spectacular movements such as *windmills, turtles, New Yorkers* and *head spins*. Sarrokh applies the Platel system: he allows everyone to improvise, perform their own story (about dance or not) and then starts work himself, using whatever comes his way. He stimulates and provokes: he has a ballerina break-dance and a break-dancer perform to baroque music. The clash of cultures becomes more intense. Sarrokh's *Carte blanche* has been much applauded. More than one hundred performances have been enjoyed throughout Europe. In 1997 *Carte blanche* was awarded the Signaal Prize for best youth production. Because of its diversity of style, the provocative inclusion of break-dance, but principally the high adrenaline level of the performance, *Carte blanche* attracted a young audience, including many immigrants; an audience who would normally never visit a theatre. Theatres view this as a welcome opportunity to pull in a new audience.

There is an urgent need for structure: *Hush Hush Hush* is the name of the company that was to see to the cultural shift on the dance scene from then on. A year later *Hush Hush Hush*'s operations were subsidised and a second production opened. Rik Verstrepen composed music for *Via*, writing for instrumentalists and a DJ! And not just any DJ: Grazzhoppa, at that time a rising star, who was seen again in a dance production by Anne Teresa de Keersmaeker.

K'Dar is an important concept in Islam: destiny. The universal question about the delicate balance between fate and free choice revolves around it. Man is always free to choose. This sometimes requires daring. *K'Dar* also conveys the idea of 'daring'. In his *K'Dar,* Sarrokh alludes to dictatorships and reveals how young people today defy their destiny, without being able to dissociate themselves from their fate.

In his next work he continues to observe social structures and hold them up for discussion. By way of the gangsta rapper Tupac Amaru Shakur, he tackles the mind of the immigrant who wants to integrate into the culture in which he has grown up but nevertheless remains attached to his deeply-anchored roots. But someone who is physically handicapped who wants to belong to the group, and a secretary who wants to be accepted into the break-dancers' milieu also have a hard time, in short: anyone who is different in any respect has adjustment problems. All of us, in fact.

How does such a process of adjustment work out? How far does toleration stretch? What forces whirl around in your body and mind and where do they lead? Aggression? Creativity? With these questions at the back of his mind Sarrokh approached the dancers for *2Pack*. The *Hush Hush Hush* dancers were not chosen for their skills, but for what they had to say. Their ideas, stories, movements, that is the raw material of Sarrokh's work. This is where he focuses his mind. This indicates the right setting for the performance. This topic was then entrusted to the dancers. Their languages, both verbal and in dance, are different, just like their cultural backgrounds. During rehearsals Dutch, English and French are tangled together. Everyone survives in a culture or subculture which is foreign to him in one way or another and has to struggle to be accepted. That makes you both vulnerable

K'Dar, 1998

Photo B. de Grove

and strong. Wonderful things can happen but there can also be conflict. This is where Sarrokh comes in: the meetings, clashes, misunderstandings, the symbioses of all those bodies with their physical and emotional memories, with their perfections and imperfections.

If the body, as a witness to emotion, was the major driving force in his former work, Sarrokh nevertheless continues to be unswervingly fascinated by the body itself and in *Bobo in Paradise* (2002) he views even more attentively and with greater wonder the purely mechanical, bio-dynamic qualities of all those diverse dancing bodies that he brings together once again.

ABDELAZIZ SARROKH
Tangier (Morocco), b. 1972

EDUCATION AND CAREER
Studied Electricity.

First employed as social worker in Ghent.
Initially led his own dance group, *Al Fath*. Danced for *Les Ballets C de la B* and in 1995 presented the first performance by his ad hoc company *Hush Hush Hush*.

WORKS
Carte blanche, 1995; *Via*, 1997; *K'Dar*, 1998; *SAD*, 2000; *2Pack*, 2000; *Dancing in the Street*, 2001; *Bobo in Paradise*, 2002

BIBLIOGRAPHY
Katie Verstockt, 'Break Dance van de straat naar het theater', in *De Scène*, XIL, 1998, no. 1, pp. 4-5.

ADDRESS
Hush Hush Hush, Cultureel Centrum Berchem
Driekoningenstraat 126, B-2600 Antwerpen (Berchem)
Tel.: +32 (0)3 286 88 20
Fax: +32 (0)3 286 88 44
info@ccbe.be
www.hushhushhush.be

Dance Organisations

KONINKLIJK BALLET VAN VLAANDEREN

In 1969 the dance pioneer Jeanne Brabants created an independent Flemish dance company for Antwerp. She became the director of the *Ballet van Vlaanderen* and André Lecleir, a former Béjart dancer, was its first choreographer.

Brabants, a consummate disciple of the 'modern' Central European principles of expression, nevertheless guided the new *Ballet* in a classical direction. Historical works by such major figures of dance history as Michel Fokine, August Bournonville and Marius Petipa were joined on the bill by modern-classical choreographers of the twentieth century, such as George Balanchine, Kurt Jooss, John Butler, Frederick Ashton, Antony Tudor, Agnes de Mille and Birgit Cullberg, 'the neighbours' who were slightly more innovative, such as Hans van Manen, Rudi van Dantzig, Nils Christe, Jiří Kylián and Maurice Béjart, and of course by the creations of Lecleir and Brabants herself. The young dancers in the group were given the opportunity to launch themselves: Aimé de Lignière (later director of the *Hogeschool voor Dans* (Dance College)), Marc Bogaerts and Danny Rosseel (now the company choreographer and deputy director).

When Brabants retired in 1984, she was succeeded by the Russian-Israeli choreographer Valery Panov, who had the *Ballet* dance his own creations. A year later a musical department was established (headed by Linda Lepomme). In 1987 Panov was succeeded by the Antwerper Robert Denvers, a former soloist and deputy director at the *Ballet van de XXste Eeuw* and a soloist at the National Ballet of Canada, but best known as a teacher and specialist in the Balanchine repertoire.

Denvers raised the *Ballet van Vlaanderen* to the top rank. It was even given its own theatre. The programme again included classical and contemporary classical work (including Rudolf Nureyev's *Don Quichote*). In 2002 Jan Fabre created a version of *Swan Lake* for the now 'Royal' *Ballet van Vlaanderen*. The success of this joint venture led to new plans for the future.

BIBLIOGRAPHY

Rina Barbier, 'Dertig jaar Ballet', in Jan Robert (ed.), *Het Koninklijk Ballet van Vlaanderen: 30 jaar ballet, 15 jaar musical*, Lannoo, Tielt, 1999.

ADDRESS

Kattendijkdok-Westkaai 16, B-2000 Antwerpen
Tel.: +32 (0)3 234 34 38
Fax: +32 (0)3 233 58 92
balletvanvlaanderen@kbvv.be
www.koninklijkballetvanvlaanderen.be

KAAITHEATER

The *Kaaitheater* in Brussels is a fine example of the arts centre model that developed in Flanders. It is a place, a house, a theatre, that was first created around an
exciting generation of performing artists and which then constantly redefined and
reoriented itself in accordance with these artists' development.

The origins of the *Kaaitheater* lie in *vzw Schaamte*, a unique form of collaboration
between artists which from the late 1970s, under the leadership of Hugo de Greef,
laid the foundations for the so-called 'Flemish wave'. What was so unique about it
was that the artists themselves owned the organisation and that one artist's
creation was financed by the income from the others' tours.

In 1977, the *Kaaitheater* was set up to operate parallel to *Schaamte*, originally as
a biennial festival that presented its own pool of artists in an international setting in
the backyard of the fossilised *Koninklijke Vlaamse Schouwburg* in Brussels. In 1987,
after five festivals, it was replaced by a programme that continued through the year
and it merged with *Schaamte*. It also acquired its own space for production and
performances, first in the *Kaaitheaterstudios* and from 1993 in the *Lunatheater*,
which in 2002 was rechristened the *Kaaitheater*.

In 1998, after more than 20 years, Hugo de Greef handed over the artistic
leadership to Johan Reyniers, who in his turn introduced a new generation of
choreographers, several of whom belong to the so-called 'conceptual movement'
that has been gaining international acclaim since the mid-nineties.

BIBLIOGRAPHY

Ritsaert ten Cate, Jef de Roeck, Luk van den Dries, Pol Arias, Wim van Gansbeke, *Humus. Vijf-
tien jaar Kaaitheater / Les quinze ans du Kaaitheater / Fifteen Years of the Kaaitheater*, Stichting
Kunstboek - Kaaitheater, Bruges - Brussels, 1993.
Peter Anthonissen, *Humus 2*, Kaaitheater, Brussels, 1998.

ADDRESS
Akenkaai 2, B-1000 Brussel
Tel.: +32 (0)2 201 58 58
Fax: +32 (0)2 201 59 65
info@kaaitheater.be
www.kaaitheater.be

KUNSTENCENTRUM VOORUIT

Since its establishment in 1982, *Kunstencentrum Vooruit*, housed in the monumental and historic *Feestlokaal Vooruit*, the former cultural centre of the *Vooruit* socialist cooperative, has had two missions: the restoration and reuse of the building and the development of its own contemporary performing arts activities. As part of the latter, music, dance and new forms of music theatre have enjoyed positive discrimination since the early nineteen-nineties.

In reference to the eclectic architecture of the building, dance programme officer Guy Cools showed the variety of styles and genres in the contemporary dance world. In 1993, Alain Platel's *Les Ballets C de la B* became the resident dance company. From its base at *Vooruit*, it has developed its own anarchistic and surrealistic form of dance theatre. But a number of Flemish and international exponents of the Anglo-American pure 'abstract dance' are also shown in contrast to this dominant local 'school'. In addition, *Vooruit* regularly zooms in on a number of foreign dance biotopes which, just like Brussels, have been important epicentres for dance innovation since the 1980s: Barcelona, Montreal and London.

Since 2001 the artistic team has been joined by Barbara Raes, in a series of interdisciplinary projects that use the whole *Vooruit* building as a location, introducing a generation of choreographers and multimedia artists who are exploring the boundaries between dance, performance and installations: live and virtual, and in both the performing and visual arts.

ADDRESS
Sint-Pietersnieuwstraat 23, B-9000 Gent
Tel.: +32 (0)9 267 28 20
Fax: +32 (0)9 267 28 30
info@vooruit.be
www.vooruit.be

Parts

The *Performing Arts Research and Training Studios (PARTS)* dance course was established in 1995 to provide a pool of trained dancers. It is a joint initiative by the *Rosas* company (Anne Teresa de Keersmaeker) and the Brussels opera house, *De Munt* (Bernard Foccroulle). De Keersmaeker is its director, and she compiles the syllabus herself.

PARTS offers a postgraduate course in contemporary dance divided into two sections (*Training* and *Research*) of two years each. The students receive training in technique and a general theoretical education that enables them to think and operate as independent creative artists. Dance is not seen as an isolated discipline. A great deal of attention is paid to other art forms such as music and theatre. Musical analysis, for example, was initially taught by the legendary Fernand Schirren, De Keersmaeker's former teacher at *Mudra*.

PARTS is emphatically international. The teachers come from several European countries and the United States and from companies led by such choreographers as Trisha Brown, William Forsythe and Pina Bausch. Among the students one encounters more than twenty nationalities every year. The contact with various cultures and views on dance provides the students with an artistic enrichment that is not to be underestimated. In order to increase the career potential and the chance of international contacts even more, the *Départs* project was launched in 2001, a joint venture involving *PARTS* and leading dance organisations in several countries, including France, Germany, Austria and Portugal.

Address

Van Volxemlaan 164, B-1190 Brussel
Tel.: +32 (0)2 344 55 98
Fax: +32 (0)2 343 53 52
mail@parts.be
www.rosas.be/parts

Dans in Kortrijk

In 1994, the civic theatre in Kortrijk, the *Limelight* arts centre and the *vzw Stella Rossa* transformed their collaboration on contemporary dance into a new, independent organisation called *Dans in Kortrijk*. In its first few seasons it brought together the productions and coproductions of *Limelight*, with dancers including Yurgen Schoora and Karin Vyncke, the dance education activities of *vzw Stella Rossa* and the various partners' activities in hosting dance, including an emphasis on choreographers from 'the south' (Italy, Portugal and Spain) who elsewhere often work in artistic 'exile'.

In 1997 *Dans in Kortrijk* became the third Flemish dance organisation to be recognised and subsidised by the Flemish Community. After a difficult start-up period, in which the artistic director Ida de Vos primarily zoomed in on the Brussels dance scene, which was not given sufficient chance in its own city, she was succeeded in 1998 by Koen Kwanten, who had for years led the production department of *Klapstuk*. Thanks to his international contacts, it took him only a few years to develop *Dans in Kortrijk* into a dynamic workshop that is a good example of the increasing internationalisation of the Flemish dance world since the second half of the nineties.

As a workshop, the accent is mainly on giving production and coproduction support to young choreographers. To this end it has at its disposal the superb studios in the *Tack Tower*, part of an old brewery that Stéphane Beel converted into a production centre for the performing arts. The results of this workshop's operations are shown together in the six-monthly *Dans@tack* events.

Address

Schouwburgplein 14, B-8500 Kortrijk
Tel.: +32 (0)56 22 89 22
Fax: +32 (0)56 22 93 93
post@dansinkortrijk.be
www.dansinkortrijk.be

STUK / KLAPSTUK

As an initiative of the *Kunstencentrum Stuk* in Leuven and the *Festival van Vlaande-ren*, the *Klapstukfestival* has always been closely linked to Leuven university and its student movement. *Klapstuk* has been the most important contemporary dance festival in Flanders since it was established in 1983. It has passed through three phases in its twenty years.

The first three festivals, led by Michel Uytterhoeven, were mainly intended to present the 'Flemish wave', in the frame of reference of the major international movements: the American postmodernists, German dance theatre, Japanese *butoh* dance and several leading French choreographers.

From the second half of the 1980s this international representation was increasingly taken over by others, such as *Kunstencentrum deSingel* in Antwerp and the *Paleis voor Schone Kunsten* (PSK) in Brussels. *Klapstuk* metamorphosed into a place for creation, devoting more attention to Belgian work and the youngest generation of choreographers. Under the artistic leadership of Bruno Verbergt (from 1988) and Johan Reyniers (from 1995), the festival expanded into activities that continued throughout the year.

In 1998 the reins of artistic leadership were taken up by An-Marie Lambrechts and Griet van Laer, who have worked on the continued integration of the all-year work of *Kunstencentrum Stuk* and the festival operations of *Klapstuk*. In 1999 and 2001 they called in Alain Platel as guest curator. In January 2002 they moved into a new building in the former *Arenberginstituut* laboratory, splendidly converted by the architect Willem-Jan Neutelings, where all the rehearsal and performance spaces were for the first time under one roof and integration was thereby achieved.

BIBLIOGRAPHY
Stuc / Stuk Werk, Kunstencentrum vzw, Leuven, 2002.

ADDRESS
Naamsestraat 96, B-3000 Leuven
Tel.: +32 (0)16 320 300
Fax: +32 (0)16 320 300
stuk@stuk.be
www.stuk.be

DE BEWEEGING (ZIMMER)

The successes of Anne Teresa de Keersmaeker, Jan Fabre and the international programme of the *Klapstukfestival* (1983) lit the fuse of Belgian dance creativity. Young artists of movement appeared everywhere, but there was nowhere for them to go. In 1984 Herbert Reymer and Bart Patoor, together with Christophe Vermeyen, annoyed by this situation, organised a festival at the *Cultuurcentrum Berchem / Antwerpen*, to show work by young Belgians in the field of movement. It was called *De Beweeging*. There was no money, but there was a stage and a curious audience. The creations were still immature and fragile, but certainly controversial: starting from a blank sheet, they were not associated with anything and they did not even react against the past. No one was able to pay for professional dancers. The artistic message was at the forefront and surprises were legion.

Herbert Reymer found a building for them, with studios and a small theatre. Young movers can now develop and show their work all year round. Mime, performance and dance: Reymer wants to sweep away the boundaries between these disciplines. Government subsidies stimulated the professionalisation of *De Beweeging* and of many companies. Numerous people were given a boost by *De Beweeging*: Alain Platel, Marc Vanrunxt, Eric Raeves, Karin Vyncke, Nicole Mossoux, José Besprosvany, Thierry Smits and so many others who have helped shape the appearance of dance in Belgium. New festival formats and programme contents keep track of the changing situation in the field. There are now plenty of workshops and theatres that support and show up and coming talent.

The mission appears to have been accomplished. Herbert Reymer left his post as director in 2001. A year later he was succeeded by Barbara van Lint, its name was changed to *Zimmer* and its course was changed in the direction of theatre.

BIBLIOGRAPHY
Steven de Belder, *De Beweeging 1984-2001*, De Beweeging, Antwerp, 2001.

ADDRESS
Gasstraat 90, B-2060 Antwerpen
Tel.: +32 (0)3 225 10 66
Fax: +32 (0)3 225 21 35
mail@wpzimmer.be
www.wpzimmer.be